"It is always enlightening to listen to a conversation among scholars who care deeply about a topic, take strikingly different positions, and engage each other in considerate and substantive ways. That's just what *God and the Problem of Evil* provides: a stimulating conversation. Well-known proponents of five distinct approaches to the most vexing of philosophical and theological topics—*Why is there suffering in God's world?*—summarize their positions in clear, accessible ways. Then each shows just how his view compares to the others. The positions presented cover a broad spectrum, yet each addresses with urgency both the intellectual and personal challenges that evil presents. The book makes a valuable contribution to current considerations of the topic."

Richard Rice, Loma Linda University, author of *Suffering and the Search for Meaning*

D1127958

SPECTRUM MULTIVIEW BOOKS

GOD AND THE PROBLEM OF EVIL

FIVE VIEWS

EDITED BY CHAD MEISTER
and JAMES K. DEW JR.

CONTRIBUTIONS BY
Phillip Cary, William Lane Craig, William Hasker,
Thomas Jay Oord, and Stephen Wykstra

IVP Academic

An imprint of InterVarsity Press
Downers Grove, Illinois

InterVarsity Press
P.O. Box 1400, Downers Grove, IL 60515-1426
ivpress.com
email@ivpress.com

InterVarsity Press® is the book-publishing division of InterVarsity Christian Fellowship/USA®, a movement of students and faculty active on campus at hundreds of universities, colleges, and schools of nursing in the United States of America, and a member movement of the International Fellowship of Evangelical Students. For information about local and regional activities, visit intervarsity.org.

All Scripture quotations, unless otherwise indicated, are taken from THE HOLY BIBLE, NEW INTERNATIONAL VERSION®, NIV® Copyright © 1973, 1978, 1984, 2011 by Biblica, Inc.™ Used by permission. All rights reserved worldwide.

Figure 1: Used by permission of Mission Frontiers *magazine published by Frontier Ventures. The chart originally appeared in the November 1990 edition of* Mission Frontiers *on page 18.*

Cover design: David Fassett
Interior design: Jeanna Wiggins
Images: © Clayton Bastiani / Trevillion Images

ISBN 978-0-8308-4024-3 (print)
ISBN 978-0-8308-9174-0 (digital)

Printed in the United States of America ∞

 As a member of the Green Press Initiative, InterVarsity Press is committed to protecting the environment and to the responsible use of natural resources. To learn more, visit greenpressinitiative.org.

Library of Congress Cataloging-in-Publication Data
A catalog record for this book is available from the Library of Congress.

P 29 28 27 26 25 24 23 22 21 20 19 18 17 16 15 14 13 12 11 10 9 8 7 6 5 4 3 2 1

Y 42 41 40 39 38 37 36 35 34 33 32 31 30 29 28 27 26 25 24 23 22 21 20 19 18 17

Contents

Introduction

CHAD MEISTER AND JAMES K. DEW JR.

Evil abounds. Regardless of when or where we look—in the feudal systems of the Middle Ages or the cyber world of the twenty-first century, in the posh suburbs of a major city or the poor slums found across the globe, in the practice of organized crime or the peccancy in organized religion—in all times and in all places we find pain, we find suffering, we find evil. Evil is no less present, no less pernicious, and no less perplexing in the modern world than it has ever been. This poses a tenacious problem for those who believe in a God who is perfectly good and loving, all-powerful, and infinitely smart. For surely a God who is good and loving would not want there to be widespread pain and suffering in the world. And surely a God who is omniscient and omnipotent could ensure that no such world would exist. But such a world does exist. Our world.

In a world like ours, the adherents of traditional theism face the burden of attempting to offer a reasoned response to this problem of evil. At least the editors and contributors of this book believe that theists face such a burden, and that is why we have crafted it. By "traditional theism" we are referring to the conventional view of God historically held within the Judeo-Christian faith. On this view God is generally understood to be personal (or at least not less than a person: one who possesses mind and will, has goals and plans and purposes, and so on), ultimate reality (the source and ground of all things), distinct from the world yet actively involved in the world (creator and sustainer), and worthy of worship (wholly good, having inherent moral perfection, and excelling in power). This theistic concept of God includes a cluster of properties, and the ones most relevant to our discussion of evil are omnibenevolence, omnipotence, and omniscience. It is important to note that there are intramural debates within Christian theism about the meanings of these attributes. Some of these debates are reflected in the contributions to this volume. Yet all of the contributors affirm the grand wisdom, knowledge, goodness, and power of the God of historic Christianity.

We (the editors) have chosen five leading Christian thinkers who embrace five different perspectives to present in clear and accessible prose what they take to be the best way to respond to what is called "the problem of evil." Before exploring their responses to the matter, it will be helpful to cover some of the relevant background material and major terms and concepts involved in the contemporary discussion on the subject.

To begin, what does the term *evil* connote? *Evil* is not an easy term to define in a precise and comprehensive manner. It is used in such diverse ways that one might wonder whether there truly is a singular meaning that captures each and every example of its usage. One might say, for example, that Joseph Stalin was an evil man, that the 2004 tsunami in Indonesia was an evil event, that an ISIS prison is an evil place, and that evolution in the animal kingdom ("nature red in tooth and claw," to quote the poet Alfred Lord Tennyson) is an evil process. But what is an accurate meaning of the term *evil* that covers each of these examples and the countless others that could be included? Lexicons and dictionaries offer little help in this way by telling us, for example, that *evil* is "the opposite of good" or "that which is morally reprehensible." Here, as with many other instances, the standard dictionary definition of the term falls short of capturing the depth, complexities, and variegations of the way the term is actually used. (A similar problem exists with the word *good*, for one might have a good pet, a good dinner, a good relationship, a good job, and a good God.)

While a useful, specific definition of the term *evil* might elude us, we can still have a sense of what we are talking about when we use it in various contexts. General descriptions such as those mentioned above can prove helpful. David Hume provides a few more: "Were a stranger to drop on a sudden into this world, I would show him, as a specimen of its ills [that is, its evils], a hospital full of disease, a prison crowded with malefactors and debtors, a field of battle strewed with carcasses, a fleet foundering in the ocean, a nation languishing under tyranny, famine, or pestilence."[1] The list of evils is endless, and it includes such broad notions as pain (physical states in which one wishes his or her circumstances were otherwise), suffering (mental states in which one wishes his or her circumstances were otherwise), and injustice (unfairness, the violation of the rights of others, and uncorrected abuse, neglect, or malfeasance).

Beyond these general categories and examples, there are also classifications of evil. A standard classification divides evil into two types: moral and natural. *Moral evils* are those evils that are in some sense the result of a person who is morally blameworthy of the resultant evil. There was intention behind the event, and the person's free will was involved. Some moral evils are very great, as in the horror of child abuse. Other examples include genocide, torture, and other terrors inflicted on humans (or perhaps other animals) by other humans. There are also less severe types of moral evils, such as stealing or speaking very negatively about someone. Furthermore, certain defects in one's character are also often counted as moral evils, including dishonesty, greed, and gluttony.

The second category of evil has to do with naturally occurring events or disasters rather than with moral agents. Examples of *natural evils* include hurricanes, tornadoes, earthquakes, tsunamis, famine, illnesses such as leukemia and Alzheimer's disease, disabilities such as deafness and blindness, and other terrible events that do harm to humans and other living creatures but for which no personal agent is responsible. Consider the tsunami noted above that occurred in Indonesia. Because of that event, over 250,000 people died. Countless others were left homeless or without fathers, mothers, siblings, and other loved ones. In times past such instances of uncontrollable natural forces have often been referred to as "acts of God" (notably in insurance claims), though more recently they are often referred to as "acts of nature." In any case, such events are natural in the sense that no human person is culpable for them, and they are evil in the sense that harm was incurred to humans or other animals.

In this book we are concerned with responses to arguments from evil—arguments that attempt to show that belief in God is unreasonable. Such

---

[1]David Hume, *Dialogues Concerning Natural Religion* (London: Penguin, 1990), 106.

arguments generally begin by pinpointing some broad class of evils, or some particular evil or set of evils, and then presenting premises that point to the penultimate conclusion that a good, wise, and all-powerful God would not have allowed for there to be such evils. This leads to the final conclusion that, since such evils do exist, God does not exist (or at least it is likely that God does not exist).

As the phrase is used in the literature, "the problem of evil" has taken many forms. Consequently, it is probably more accurate to speak of *problems of evil*, as there are various difficulties we are confronted with given evil's reality. Nevertheless, what is generally taken to be the heart of the problem can be put simply in standard logical form as follows:

If God exists, then evil should not exist.
Evil does exist.
Therefore, God does not exist.

The problem is that there seems to be an inconsistency between God's nature and the reality of evil. As ancient Greek philosopher Epicurus (341–270 BC) put it: "Either God wants to abolish evil, and cannot; or he can, but does not want to. If he wants to, but cannot, he is impotent. If he can, but does not want to, he is wicked. If God can abolish evil, and God really wants to do it, why is there evil in the world?"[2]

There are two primary approaches in responding to arguments from evil. One approach, referred to as a *theodicy* (which comes from an ancient Greek term that means "a justification of God"), attempts to offer an account that demonstrates that God has a good reason or set of reasons for allowing or not preventing what appears to be the evil in question. A second approach, generally referred to as a *defense*, does not claim to provide an actual reason or set of reasons for God's allowing or not preventing evil. Instead, it attempts to rebut the argument from evil in a different way, such as by controverting one or more of the premises in the argument. A defense takes on less of a burden than a theodicy, for it is not proposing a solution to the problem of evil, nor offering a justification for any particular evil or set of

---

[2]Epicurus, according to Lactantius (ca. AD 240–ca. 320) in *De Ira Dei* (*On the Wrath of God*). An online translation of the work by Philip Schaff can be found at *Documenta Catholica Omnia*, 2006, www.documentacatholicaomnia.eu/03d/0240-0320,_Lactantius,_De_Ira_Dei_%5BSchaff%5D ,_EN.pdf, page 409 in the text.

evils. With the exception of Stephen Wykstra, the contributors in this book are attempting to provide a theodicy (though Craig's essay could also be construed as a defense). In other words, they are not merely trying to rebut the problem of evil. They are taking on the burden of providing a possible justification for why God allows or does not prevent evil.

Above we have sketched some of the main issues that are relevant to arguments from evil, laying out the terrain, clarifying some key terms, and introducing some of the general themes and relevant topics in the discussion that follows. Our authors are some of the leading thinkers today on God and evil. Each will first present an essay arguing for his view with respect to the problem of evil, then follow with a response to the other four authors' views on the problem.

The first essay is written by Phillip Cary. He is professor of philosophy and scholar in residence at the Templeton Honors College at Eastern University. He is an Augustine scholar and has published many articles and books, including the trilogy *Augustine's Invention of the Inner Self: The Legacy of a Christian Platonist*; *Inner Grace: Augustine in the Traditions of Plato and Paul*; and *Outward Signs: The Powerlessness of External Things in Augustine's Thought*, all published by Oxford University Press (2000, 2008, and 2008, respectively). In his chapter, "The Classic View," he articulates and defends what we are referring to in this book as the classic view of God and evil. It is classic in that its general contours can be traced back to that early medieval thinker who is widely considered to be the most influential theologian of early Western Christianity: fifth-century African bishop Augustine of Hippo (AD 354–430). As Professor Cary notes, the features of the position he develops were held not only by Augustine but also by such later luminaries as Thomas Aquinas, Julian of Norwich, Martin Luther, John Calvin, C. S. Lewis, and John Paul II. What is at stake for Augustine and others who held to the classic view is not so much "the problem of evil" as delineated above, but rather the related problem of wondering how evil can exist *on the assumption* that God is omnipotent, omnibenevolent, and so on. The classic reply is that evil occurs because God permits it, and God does so because of a greater good that derives from it.

The classic view sees the grand narrative of world history as one that begins with Adam's fall and culminates with Christ's return. It has a beneficent beginning, in which God creates everything good, and it has a beneficent ending, in which Christ restores all things (with the exception of the damned) to perfection. What is between the beginning and the end—the sin, suffering, and corruption manifest in the world—might seem to have no meaning or purpose or goal, but we have the hope, through the gospel of Christ, that a greater good will come out of it all.

The second essay is by William Lane Craig. He is research professor of philosophy at Talbot School of Theology and professor of philosophy at Houston Baptist University. His many publications include *God Over All: Divine Aseity and the Challenge of Platonism* (Oxford University Press, 2016); *Time and Eternity: Exploring God's Relationship to Time* (Crossway, 2001); and *The Only Wise God: The Compatibility of Divine Foreknowledge and Human Freedom* (Baker, 1987). In his essay, "A Molinist View," he articulates a Molinist perspective, based on the work of Jesuit theologian Luis de Molina (1535–1600) and his theory of divine providence. Molina, a leading figure in the sixteenth-century revival of scholasticism, argued that God's comprehensive providence over the created order is in keeping with free human actions and that God's infallible foreknowledge of and causal influence on events in the world (including free human actions) does not necessarily determine what those events will be.

Central to the Molinist view is divine middle knowledge in God's deliberations regarding the creation. Logically prior to his decree to create the world, God possesses different kinds of knowledge. Natural knowledge is God's knowledge of all possible worlds. Free knowledge is God's knowledge of the actual world. Between them is middle knowledge—God's knowledge of what every possible free creature would do under any possible set of circumstances, including which possible worlds God can make actual. This provides God with knowledge of all true counterfactual propositions of creaturely freedom (such as what the outcome of the next national election will be). So how does Molinism help to address the problem of evil? Craig argues that it is relevant to various versions of the problem: the probabilistic version of the internal problem of evil (which claims that the evil and suffering in the world make it highly improbable, if not impossible, that God exists), the external problem of evil (that the apparently pointless and unnecessary evils in the world constitute *evidence* against God's existence), and the emotional problem of evil (which concerns how to extirpate the emotional antipathy people have toward a God who would permit such evil).

The third essay is by William Hasker. He is emeritus professor of philosophy at Huntington College. He has published many books and articles, including *The Triumph of God over Evil* (IVP Academic, 2008); *Providence, Evil, and the Openness of God* (Routledge, 2004); and *God, Time, and Knowledge* (Cornell University Press, 1998). In his essay, "An Open Theist View," he presents a theodicy that is consistent with open theism in that it works within the framework of a dynamic, relational conception of a God who takes risks.

Hasker distinguishes between what he calls a general-policy theodicy, one that justifies God's permitting certain evils that are the consequence of a general policy that an omniscient and omnibenevolent God might adopt, and a specific-benefit theodicy, which would require that each individual instance of evil lead to a greater good, or to the prevention of an equal or greater evil. He develops two forms of a general-policy theodicy, a natural order theodicy, which accounts for natural evil, and a free will theodicy, which accounts for moral evil. The two theodicies parallel each other in that for each of them the world consists of the sorts of features a good and wise Creator might well have chosen, but also that such features lead to consequences of moral and natural evil. Even so, he argues, the creation of our world was well worth it.

The next essay is by Thomas Oord. He is professor of theology and philosophy at Northwest Nazarene University. He has also written many articles and books, including *The Uncontrolling Love of God: An Open and Relational Account of Providence* (IVP Academic, 2015); *Defining Love: A Philosophical, Scientific, and Theological Engagement* (Brazos, 2010); and *The Nature of Love: A Theology* (Chalice Press, 2010). In his essay, titled "An Essential Kenosis View," he presents what he calls the essential kenosis solution to the problem of evil. The word *kenōsis* is a Greek term found in various places in the New Testament that literally means "emptiness." The scriptural passage most relevant to the issue is Philippians 2:3-7. This kenosis passage, notes Oord, suggests that Jesus reveals God's power to be one of persuasion, not one of coercion. Jesus "made himself nothing [emptied himself] by taking the very nature of a servant." His power is others-oriented and demonstrates servant love rather than controlling love. It is this loving nature of God that provides us with a solution to the problem of evil.

Oord's solution includes five dimensions: the empathetic, didactic, therapeutic, strategic, and sovereignty. According to the last dimension, which he develops most fully in his essay, in order for God to prevent evil unilaterally, God would have to deny his own loving, self-giving, others-empowering, and necessarily uncontrolling nature. A God with such a nature would not override the freedom and existence of others, nor would he override the freedom and regularities of the natural world, which God created. In other words, because of the uncontrolling love of God, God cannot prevent genuine evil unilaterally.

The final essay is by Stephen Wykstra. He is professor of philosophy at Calvin College. He has published numerous articles in leading philosophy journals and prominent academics presses, including the *International Journal for the Philosophy of Religion*, *Faith and Philosophy*, *Philo*, Oxford University Press, and Cornell University Press. His essay is titled "A Skeptical Theism View." The term *skeptical theism* is an unfortunate one, for it might seem to connote a skeptical attitude about the belief that God exists. That is not how the term is used in the literature. As Wykstra notes, there are many versions of skeptical theism, but there are two elements that unite them all. First, if the God of theism does exist (which most skeptical theists affirm), then we should not expect to understand much about God's purposes or actions in the world. And second, if the first point is true, then what appears to be strong evidence against theism is not very strong after all. In his essay he does more than provide a philosophical argument for skeptical theism and delineate its strengths and limits. He provides stories—real stories that capture the heart as well as the mind and expose some of the "deeper roots" of the issue.

After first sharing three pithy stories, he expounds on the classic paper titled "The Evidential Problem of Evil," from which skeptical theism derived. He then sets forth the core of skeptical theism and explains his own (now famous) criterion for evaluating certain sorts of claims, such as those given in the evidential problem of evil. He calls his criterion CORNEA—an acronym for the "Condition Of ReasoNable Epistemic Access"—and demonstrates its relevance to the evidential problem. His argument, he maintains, removes the sting from at least some of the evidential arguments on offer. In the next portion of the essay, he proposes new directions for skeptical theism—some new ways forward that might seem to contradict the very essence of skeptical theism as it has traditionally been understood.

We are grateful to each of the contributors—Phillip Cary, William Lane Craig, William Hasker, Thomas Oord, and Stephen Wykstra—for their valuable contributions and for their congeniality and collegiality in crafting this book. We are also appreciative of our IVP editor, David Congdon, who offered assistance and insight from the very beginning of this project. And we are beholden to our wives, Tara Dew and Tammi Meister, and to our families for their unrelenting encouragement, patience, and support.

Now on to the arguments!

PART ONE

PERSPECTIVES
ON THE
PROBLEM OF EVIL

1

A Classic View

PHILLIP CARY

The classic view of evil in the Christian tradition derives from the way the church fathers read Scripture. An especially important church father is Augustine of Hippo, the fifth-century African bishop who is the most influential theologian in the West outside the Bible itself. This chapter will present features of the classic view that are widely shared within the broad Augustinian tradition, which includes thinkers as diverse as Thomas Aquinas, Julian of Norwich, Martin Luther, John Calvin, C. S. Lewis, and John Paul II. Augustine's legacy to these thinkers is a sophisticated combination of biblical theology and ancient philosophy that remains inescapably influential today but certainly not uncontroversial.

Because the classic view has roots that go back to the ancient world of the church fathers, it does not always ask the same questions as modern thinkers. One typical modern way of stating the problem of evil, for instance, is to ask how it can be rational to believe in the existence of a God who is both good and omnipotent when there is so much evil in the world: wouldn't an omnipotent God be able to eliminate all evil, and if he were good would he not in fact do so? The classic view of evil, by contrast, typically begins with questions that go in the opposite direction: for example, assuming that God is good and omnipotent, how is evil even possible? But of course answering this question will help us answer the modern question. It will also help us with difficult pastoral questions, such as: How can we trust that an omnipotent God is good when there is so much evil in the world, including the horrible suffering of people we love? In many ways this is the most important question, because it resonates so deeply with biblical prayer.

The basic answer to the problem of evil given by the classic view is that no evil takes place unless God permits it, and that God has a good reason for permitting each evil, which takes the form of a greater good that he uses the evil to bring about. Of course this greater good principle, as it is often called, is far from a complete answer to the problem of evil. It does not tell us how to find out what is the greater good that gives meaning to each particular evil we suffer. But it does say something important about the structure of Christian hope, including the particular answers that we hope to find when, as the prayer says, the kingdom of God comes on earth as it is in heaven.

EVIL AS CORRUPTION

To see how the classic view arrives at its answers, we need to start at a different place from most modern theodicies, which tend to focus on the problem of suffering and moral evil. In the classic view, evil means something much broader than that. In part this is because in Latin, the language of Augustine and nearly all Augustinian thinkers for over a thousand years, the word for "evil" (*malum*) means "bad" as well as "evil." So English-speaking readers need to be aware that before the modern period, questions about the nature of evil concerned anything bad—anything gone wrong, anything defective, any failure. The key term for this in Augustine is *corruption* (Latin *corruptio*), which can refer to any way that things go bad.[1] C. S. Lewis captures the idea when he says "badness is only spoiled goodness."[2] A rotten apple, a ruined house, a wicked soul, a divided community are all good things that have been corrupted or spoiled, each in its own way.

The term *corruptio* was used in the Latin translation of the Bible and is reflected in the King James version of 1 Corinthians 15:53: "This corruptible must put on incorruption, and this mortal must put on immortality." In order to undo death forever, Paul is saying, the gift of everlasting life must protect our corruptible bodies from ever being corrupted. Hence

---

[1]Key discussions of evil as corruption in Augustine are *Confessions* 7.11.17–7.13.19, *Enchiridion* 3.11–4.14, and *On the Nature of the Good* 1-23. The first two texts are available in numerous editions; the third can be found in a good translation in the Library of Christian Classics series, *Augustine: Earlier Writings*, trans. John H. S. Burleigh (Philadelphia: Westminster, 1953).

[2]C. S. Lewis, *Mere Christianity* (New York: Macmillan, 1960), book 2, chap. 2 ("The Invasion").

resurrection in Christ means there is no sickness, no deformity, nothing that goes wrong with our bodies. Such permanent freedom from corruption is what Christ's victory over evil looks like in every aspect of human life, according to the classic view. It is a victory that transforms both body and soul, reversing the corruption of sin and all its ill effects. In freeing us from all corruption, the risen Lord in the end overcomes all suffering, illness of body, pain of heart, or discord of communities.

So the classic view does have a great deal to say about sin and suffering, but it puts both in a larger context, which is fundamentally ontological. Corruption means loss of form, which amounts to loss of being, a tendency toward decay, destruction, and death. When a house is thoroughly corrupted, it loses the form or structure of a house and thus fails to *be* a house: it falls into ruin and becomes no longer a house at all but a disordered heap of stone and wood and scattered materials. Likewise, when a living thing is corrupted it loses its life: a dead horse ceases to *be* a horse when it loses the form of a horse and becomes instead a pile of decaying horseflesh. Such is the destiny of all flesh, until the day comes when the corruptible puts on incorruption.

The problem of evil, in Augustinian terms, can be summed up in the question, How can there be corruption when all things are created by one omnipotent God, who is wholly good and creates nothing bad or corrupt? The first step in answering this question is to notice that corruption is not a form of being but is always a failure to be something. It is like the ruination in a half-ruined house. The house itself, insofar as it still exists, is a good thing, but the disorder and lack of structure in it is bad. So the evil itself, the ruination or corruption, has no being except as something lacking in the house—the structure and form that it is missing. Thus we can say evil exists, but it exists the way that a lack or an absence exists. It is real, but only in the way something can really be absent.

That evil has no being of its own is an important ontological point because it upholds the pure goodness of the Creator. Because God creates all things that have being, there is no kind of being that is by nature bad or evil. As Augustine puts it, quite bluntly, "Whatever things exist are good."[3] He

---

[3] Augustine, *Confessions* 7.12.18, trans. Henry Chadwick (New York: Oxford University Press, 1992).

does not mean there is no evil in the world, of course, but rather that evil always has the aspect of corruption, lack of form and being. Hence Augustine can say there are evil things in the world, but he adds that every evil thing has the character of an "evil good," or (as we could also translate his phrase) a "bad good thing."[4] There is no deep paradox in this phrase: it simply means that every bad thing is a good thing that has been to some degree corrupted, its goodness partly spoiled. Insofar as it is not wholly destroyed and still has being, it is good, like a house badly in need of repair: the house is a good thing, yet it is a bad house. In that sense it is a bad good thing, an evil good.

We can go one step further: even in a completely ruined house the wood and stones scattered about are good things, though they no longer have the goodness of being a house. Goodness, in this way, is primary and inescapable—whatever thing you look at is good in some way, though it might not have the full goodness that it could or should have. We mourn over a ruined house, because the disordered stones we see are not the house they once were. Yet the very stones and dust might be dear to us, like ruined Jerusalem (Ps 102:14).

TWO LABELS

This is not the only way of thinking about the nature of evil. It is easy to suppose, after all, that evil has a being of its own that opposes the good. This would make evil the contrary of the good, in the way that black is the contrary of white. But the classic view avoids this kind of black-and-white thinking. To put it in the sophisticated terms of medieval logic, evil is not the *contrary* of good but its *privation*.[5] The term refers to a thing being *deprived* of some good appropriate to the kind of being it is. If evil is a privation, then it is related to good the way darkness is to light, not black to white. Unlike black, which is a real color (for example, on a painter's palette), darkness is not something real in itself. It is only the absence of light or, we could say, light not being there. And to be deprived of light when it should

---

[4]Augustine, *Enchiridion* 4.13.

[5]Both the logical terminology (*privation* in contrast to *contrary* as well as mere *negation*) and the illustration (darkness and light rather than black and white) can be found in Thomas Aquinas, *Summa Theologica*, part I, question 17, article 4. The terminology is applied to the concept of evil in *Summa Theologica*, question 48, article 3.

be there is bad. Hence one common label for the classic view, stemming from this medieval terminology, is the *privative* account of the nature of evil. It means not that evil is sheer negation (as if, absurdly, whatever does not exist were evil) but rather that evil is what takes place when things are deprived of some good they ought to have.

The black-and-white style of thinking is nowadays commonly labeled *dualism*. This term can be misleading, however, because there are many kinds of dualism. The kind of dualism Augustinian theology rejects is represented most famously by the Manichaean heresy, against which Augustine wrote many of his books. This is a cosmological dualism in which the world consists of two kinds of being, good and evil. It should not be confused with soul-body dualism, which is the view that souls and bodies are two different kinds of being. Most Augustinian theologians over the centuries, though not all, have been soul-body dualists. On the other hand, most cosmological dualists, such as the Manichaeans, are also soul-body dualists, and they typically combine the two kinds of dualism by identifying bodies with the evil sort of being and souls with the good. This identification is one that Augustinian theology firmly rejects. In that sense, the classic, Augustinian view of evil is strongly antidualist.

Again confusion is possible here: Augustine can sound dualist to modern ears because he does not hesitate to say that bodies are inferior to souls. But in the hierarchical conception of the world that forms the background for Augustine's thought, *inferior* does not mean evil. The whole hierarchy of being from top to bottom is good. Hence inferior things, lower down on the scale of being, are inferior *goods*. There is nothing bad about a stone, for instance, but it is less good than living creatures, for life is a higher-level good that it lacks. Likewise, there is nothing bad in the nature of the beasts of the field, but they are less good than human beings, who are endowed with the great good of reason that beasts lack. Thus also, for an Augustinian soul-body dualist, there is nothing evil about our bodies, though they are inferior to our souls, which give them life.

WHY GOD DOES NOT HAVE TO CREATE EVIL

Since evil has no being of its own, it is not a being that God creates. This point is so fundamental for the classic view that it is worth looking at three reasons why people think otherwise and believe that God must create evil. The first two are not commonly found in the philosophical literature, but they produce enough confusion in the general discussion that they are worth examining.

First, it is sometimes said that God must create evil because without knowing evil one cannot know or appreciate what is good. From an Augustinian perspective, this is entirely backward. It is like saying you need darkness in order to see the light. But in fact you can only see a shadow and know it as a shadow by seeing the light around it, which gives the shadow what form or shape it has. The point is that the good can be known for itself, in its form and structure and beauty, while evil can only be known in light of the good it is missing. It is a point of wisdom to understand the form or structure of various kinds of evil by knowing what kind of good they are missing, and where and how. You know that a house is ruined only because you know something about what the form of a house is and should be. And you know that a person or a society is corrupt only because you have some grasp of the standard of justice that the person or society violates.

Second, it is sometimes said that in order to give us free will, God must create evil things for us to choose. On an Augustinian account, this notion is mistaken in two ways. The first mistake is to assume that free will is a neutral power, equally poised between choosing good and choosing evil. This is sometimes called the "liberty of indifference," which is to say that the difference between good and evil makes no difference in the freedom of the will. Augustinian theology, on the contrary, teaches that the will, like everything God creates, is by nature oriented toward good, not evil. Hence freedom of the will is its ability to love and choose what is good. That is what free will is for, as the eye is for seeing. To love or choose evil is of course possible, but it is not a power or ability of free will but the failure and corruption of the will, as nearsightedness is the failure to see well due to corruption of the structure of the eye. This is why Augustinian theologians such as Luther can speak of the bondage of the will. It is precisely the will, by nature free to love the good, that can be subjected to the bondage of sin, just as it is precisely the eye, by nature capable of vision, that can go blind and lose the power to see.

The second mistake is to think that choosing evil means choosing an evil thing. On an Augustinian account, moral evil does not normally mean choosing an evil thing but choosing in an evil way. Hence the grammatical form of the phrase "to choose evil" is misleading. In Augustinian discourse moral evil is, as it were, related to our choices adverbially, not as their direct object. We don't choose evil so much as choose evilly.[6] Think of how a thief chooses a car to steal. He is probably looking for a good car, not a bad one, but his way of seeking to get it is evil, because theft is an injustice. So he is not choosing something evil, but rather choosing to get a good thing in an evil way. The evil is located not in the thing he chooses but in the corruption of his own soul, the ruination of a will deprived of the justice that ought to be part of the structure of all human actions.

A third reason for thinking God must create evil stems from a philosophical criticism of the privative account of evil. Evil has a real effect on things—so the criticism goes—and if we assume that only real beings can have real causal effects, it follows that evil must be a real being. So if God created all real beings, then God must have created evil. This is a serious criticism, because the classic view shares the assumption that only real beings have real causal effects. Therefore, as Thomas Aquinas says, "Only good can be a cause, because nothing can be a cause except inasmuch as it is a being, and every being, as such, is good."[7] Yet this does not mean evil has no causal effect whatsoever, just as the privative account does not mean evil has no reality whatsoever. Rather, it means evil has no causal effect of its own, just as it has no real being of its own.

To see this point, notice the sense in which, on the privative account, there can be no such thing as pure evil. The reality of evil is the reality of an absence, like a hole in a shirt: you can't have the hole unless you have the shirt. "Pure hole"—without a shirt to put it in—makes no sense; it means nothing at all. In particular, it means nothing that plays any causal role in

---

[6]As Augustine puts it, "When the will leaves the higher and turns to the lower, it becomes bad not because the thing to which it turns is bad, but because the turning is itself perverse. It follows that it is not the inferior thing which causes the evil choice; it is the will itself . . . that desires the inferior thing in a perverted and inordinate manner." *City of God* 12.6, trans. Henry Bettenson (New York: Penguin, 1984).

[7]Aquinas, *Summa Theologica*, part I, question 49, article 1, trans. Fathers of the English Dominican Province (Westminster, MD: Christian Classics, 1981).

the world: unlike a hole in your shirt, it is nothing you could notice or do anything about, it does no harm, mars nothing, and has no presence in the world, not even the presence of an absence. In the same way, "pure evil" also makes no sense, does no harm, has no presence in the world, and has no effect on anything.

Real evil is thus always "impure": it has no reality or causal effect without the good. It is parasitic on the good, in that its reality is always the reality of something missing, defective, or deformed in things that are by nature good. Thus the causal effect of evil is a defective effect, due to the failure of a good thing to do a good job at what it does because of some impairment or deformity, like a half-ruined house that fails to provide adequate shelter or an alcoholic who is unable to do her work well. Evil takes the form of real defects with real effects, but it gets its power to do anything at all from the reality of the good things it deforms. Aquinas compares it to a man with a limp: his ability to walk is a good thing, but the deformity that makes it impossible for him to walk well is not. Likewise in a morally evil action, the ability to act at all comes from God as the Creator, who made the human will as well as the human body, but the vice that makes the action evil is a deformity of the will that is not God's doing.[8]

CORRUPTIBLE CREATURES

Since evil takes the form of corruption, we can ask: Why does God make corruption possible in the first place? Why does he make creatures that are corruptible? Augustine's answer is that if there is to be creation at all, there is no alternative to corruptible things, because all creatures are by nature corruptible. This does not mean they are inevitably corrupted, but it does mean they are inherently *capable* of being corrupted or (better put) *vulnerable* to corruption. They are corruptible precisely because they are created. Corruption and nonbeing are always a possibility for created things, for they came into being and therefore can cease to be. Every house that is built is a house that can be ruined. Only God is incorruptibly good, as he never came into being and therefore cannot possibly fail to be. He is, to use a favorite patristic term, uncreated.

---

[8]Aquinas, *Summa Theologica*, part I, question 49, article 2, reply 2.

Therefore God cannot create incorruptible beings, for God cannot create something uncreated. In other words, God cannot create God.[9] What he can do is give created beings the gift of everlasting life, preserving from corruption what is by nature corruptible. This is evidently what Paul has in mind when he says, "This corruptible must *put on* incorruption" (1 Cor 15:53 KJV). As the church fathers put it, what is *by nature* corruptible receives *by grace* an incorruptible life. The root of the nature-grace distinction here is the difference between Christ, who in his divine being is the eternal Son of God by nature, and those he redeems, who become sons and daughters of God by the grace of adoption. He who is divine by nature took up human nature and made it his own in order to share his eternal life with those who are by nature vulnerable to corruption and death. Without ceasing to be the incorruptible God, he clothes humanity in his own person with a glorious incorruption that is now available to every human being.

ORIGINS OF EVIL

Though evil is always a possibility for creatures, something has to explain why the possibility becomes actual. And because only good things can be causes, the origin of evil always lies in something good. Very often, as we have seen, it originates from something good that is already partly corrupted and isn't doing a good job, like the wounded body of a man who limps or the disordered life of an alcoholic who can't do good work. But there are two kinds of evil that can be caused by good things doing what they do well.

The first kind has to do with things that English usage usually calls "bad" rather than "evil." Often one good thing can be bad for another and corrupt it when they come into contact, as when a fire burns up wood or when cattle eat grass. In the whole order of nature, which we now call *ecology*, these kinds of corruption contribute to the good of the whole.[10] Every year the

---

[9]This is an important implication of trinitarian theology. The eternal Son of God, who is true God, is not created but eternally begotten by God the Father. In the words of the Nicene Creed, he is "begotten not created," which means he originates from the Father but has always existed. This is the basis on which the Council of Nicaea condemned the teaching that "there was once when he was not." See Philip Schaff, *The Creeds of Christendom* (New York: Harper & Row, 1932), 1:29.

[10]See Aquinas's account of how good is the cause of evil in *Summa Theologica*, part I, question 49, article 1, and cf. Augustine, *City of God* 11.22; 12.4-5.

grass withers and the flower fades, so that there can be new grass and flowers next year. Even forest fires, we have come to realize, are part of the natural cycle of renewal in many ecosystems. There is no "problem of evil" here, so long as the larger ecological scheme of things is not itself disordered.

The second kind of evil that can be caused by what is uncorrupted has the nature of punishment. Just punishment results in bad things happening to those who deserve the punishment, but it is morally good precisely because it is just. This is why Scripture can speak quite freely of God bringing evil upon people, which is to say bringing upon the wicked the bad things they deserve.[11] The Hebrew term for this is often translated by words like *disaster*, but it is in fact the standard catchall term for anything that is bad or evil—for Hebrew, like Latin, has only the one term where English has two. Thus the classic view takes divine punishment to be evil in one sense but not in another: it is a bad thing, a form of corruption and destruction (ruined cities, men and women slain, plague and famine) that is nonetheless morally good, precisely because the punishment is just. This is the one sense in which the classic view is willing to say that God directly causes evil.[12] But it is important for English speakers to bear in mind that *evil* here has the sense of something bad that is not morally evil.

DISORDERED LOVE

There is a deeper and more difficult question about the origin of evil, however, which has to do with the first moral evil or sin. (In the classic view these two terms are essentially equivalent.) The first sin does not originate from one good thing corrupting another but from a good thing corrupting itself. Here the concept of free will is central, for moral evil originates within the self as a corruption in the will. And here we must say more about the Augustinian concept of will and how it can go wrong.

The will is a good thing, because it is by nature oriented toward the good of happiness. We all want to be happy, which means we aim to attain what is best for us.[13] Happiness, in Augustinian theology as in classical philosophy,

---

[11]For a representative sample of this very frequent usage, see for example 1 Kings 9:9; Is 31:2; Jer 19:15; Ezek 14:22; Jon 3:10.

[12]See for example Aquinas, *Summa Theologica*, part I, question 49, article 2.

[13]For Augustine our wanting to be happy is not a trivial thought but the first principle of ethics and the essential nature of the will. See its fundamental role in *City of God* 10.1 and *Enchiridion* 28.105

does not mean a feeling but rather the attainment of the intrinsic purpose of one's life—not an arbitrary objective we choose for ourselves but the end or telos that is built into human nature, "the chief end of man," as the catechism puts it.[14] We could also say: happiness is *true* success in life, whatever that is. The key question indeed is what true success or happiness really is, for moral evil results when we seek happiness in the wrong way or in the wrong things.

For the Augustinian tradition there is a crucial sense in which we do not choose what makes us happy, and then another sense in which we do. For, on the one hand, we do not decide what true success in life really is. Because we are human beings made in God's image, the only ultimate happiness for us is everlasting life, which means being united with God forever in love. But, on the other hand, we do choose things that we think will make us happy. And the point here is that our choices in this regard can go wrong. We can seek happiness in things that cannot really make us happy. It's what happens in acts of lust and greed, for example. We love something other than God as if it could make us truly happy.

In Augustine's theology, all moral evil is a kind of love. It is love disordered and deformed, twisted in the wrong direction. The essence of the disorder is to love lower things in place of higher things. This is how the hierarchy of being takes on moral significance. There is no evil in the nature of inferior things, as we've seen, but to seek inferior things as if they could make us ultimately happy is both foolishness and sin. Money is a good thing, for example, but only an instrumental good. To seek any amount of money as if it were more valuable than human beings (making a profit from unjustly exploiting their labor, for example) is evil not only because of the harm it does to others but because it is in itself a disorder and corruption of the will. It loves a good thing in the wrong order, seeking to enjoy as an ultimate end what should be used for better purposes than itself. Similarly, when the Augustinian tradition voices disapproval of carnal or fleshly loves, this is not because bodily things such as food and drink are evil, but because they are inferior goods that should not be sought as ultimate ends. They are

---

(the citations could be multiplied), as well as *On the Trinity* 13.4.7, where he quotes this principle from Cicero's *Hortensius*, the text that made him a philosopher (*Confessions* 3.4.7-8).

[14]Westminster Shorter Catechism, question 1, in Schaff, *Creeds of Christendom*, 3:676.

genuinely good and often necessary for our life, but they should not be sought as if they could make us ultimately happy.

The proper order of love is given in Jesus' twofold command to love God first and then one's neighbor. For the Augustinian tradition this means to seek to be united with God as one's ultimate good, the source of everlasting happiness, and to seek the same good for one's neighbor. All other goods, including every pleasure or bodily good, come after these. Sin or moral evil originates when the will turns away from God, the supreme Good, and prefers something else in his place.

THE FIRST SIN

In a kind of thought experiment that has had a great influence on the Western tradition, Augustine treats the first sin, which is the beginning of moral evil in the world, as an act of pride in which some of the angels sinned by turning toward themselves rather than God, as if they could become the basis of their own being and happiness.[15] Their sin was to love something good—themselves—but in the wrong order, putting themselves before God. Thus they became fallen angels, which is to say devils, and fell into misery and condemnation. You could call this self-love, but it hardly deserves the name, for it means failing to seek their own highest good, which was to be found only in God, not in themselves.

(Here it is worth mentioning in passing that in Augustine's theology *selfishness* is not a very apt or illuminating name for the root of sin, because properly ordered love does mean seeking our own good. And since happiness is essentially social—ultimately it is the shared life of the community of the blessed, which Augustine calls "the city of God"—to seek our own good we must seek also the good of our neighbors.[16] Because our happiness is to be united to a supreme Good that is a common good, none of us can be happy alone. Hence love of our own happiness implies desiring happiness also for our neighbor.)

To ask how moral evil first entered the world, from an Augustinian standpoint, is to ask how evil could arise in a world that is wholly good and

---

[15] *City of God* 12.6.

[16] See the important moment in Augustine's *City of God* 19.3, when he indicates his agreement with the philosophers who say that "happy life is social, and for its own sake loves the good of friends as its own, just as it wishes for them, for their own sake, what it wishes for itself" (trans. Bettenson).

uncorrupted. Augustine's thought experiment about the fallen angels tackles this problem. There were no evil things in the world for them to choose, but they chose evilly by choosing an inferior good—themselves—in preference to God. They loved what they knew could not possibly be their highest good in preference to what they knew was their highest good. That much is clear. The deep puzzle about this choice, however, is its sheer irrationality and self-destructiveness. It amounts to a conscious rejection of their own happiness, following a desire that what they know cannot be their highest good should become their highest good. What could be the cause of such a choice, in creatures in whom there was no prior defect of understanding or will, and no evil around to corrupt them? Here Augustine's reasons give out. The most he can say at this point is that the failure to choose their own good was always a possibility, because their free will, like all good things God created, can be corrupted. But why this possibility became an actuality—why they actually sinned—is something Augustine cannot explain, and he does not try.[17] At its root moral evil must be absurd, involving a failure of intelligibility as well as a failure of being.

ADAM'S SIN

Though in its core it remains deeply irrational, human evil is more intelligible than Satan's sin in Augustine's view, for it takes place in a world in which corrupt beings, beginning with Satan and his fallen angels, have already had an effect. Thus in the traditional Augustinian reading, the serpent in the garden of Eden represents the devil offering humanity inducements to sin. Yet Augustine does not put much emphasis on the literal elements of the story, the talking serpent (which in the traditional interpretation is the devil in disguise) and the tree of knowledge (which has no magical power but is prohibited, Augustine says, as a test of obedience). These are not the really central element in the origin of human sin, which at its heart is a corruption of will very much like the devil's, based on an attempt to

---

[17]"Let no one therefore seek the efficient cause of an evil will; for it is not efficient but deficient, since the evil is not an effect but a defect. For to defect from Him who supremely is and turn to that which is inferior, is to begin to have an evil will. To want to find the causes of such defects— which are not efficient but deficient, as I said—is as if someone wanted to see darkness or hear silence, which are known to us through our eyes and ears, yet not due to their form but rather due to their lack [*privatione*] of form." *City of God* 12.7, trans. Bettenson.

make oneself the ground of one's own being and the source of one's own ultimate good.[18] Again, it is to choose a good thing—oneself—above God. It is foolishness as well as disobedience, for one's own highest good is always God, not oneself.

In the classic view, sin is the beginning of many other evils. Disordered love leads to exploitation, oppression, and war, as well as the misuse of the goods of creation and therefore all sorts of disorder in the natural world. The whole creation is subjected to evil and futility when the human creature made in God's image, who was to rule over the rest of creation (Gen 1:26), brings disorder to the earth instead of wisdom and justice. Therefore, says Paul, the creation itself must be delivered from "the bondage of corruption" (Rom 8:21—again the King James Version reflects the Latin *corruptio*). For it was subjected to evil and futility *in hope*, as Paul insists (Rom 8:20), and therefore it awaits, along with humanity, the glorious liberty of the children of God when they are freed from corruption.

DIVINE PERMISSION

With Adam we enter a story that moves from corruption and death at the beginning to glory and everlasting life at the end, when all good things are restored in Christ (Rom 5:12-21; cf. Acts 3:21). There are a great many ways of telling this story within the Bible itself and within the Augustinian tradition as well, some of which go further than Augustine in deemphasizing the literal elements of the initial episode in the garden of Eden. I will not tell one particular version of the story but present some general features. Most important, for the classic view, is the greater-good principle. It is the twofold teaching that (1) no evil happens without God's permission, and (2) God always has a good reason for permitting the evils that happen, because he uses every evil to bring about a greater good.

The greater-good principle is nowadays highly controversial. To begin with, the first part of the principle assumes a very strong view of divine sovereignty, which recent philosophers have called "meticulous providence." It's meticulous because it has God involved in all the details. Under this view of providence, every particular evil is one God could have prevented but

---

[18]*City of God* 14.11-13.

freely chose to permit. So it is not just that he permits certain *kinds* of evil in order to promote or safeguard certain kinds of good. Still less does it mean that he *must* permit these evils for the sake of these goods.

For example, the argument is sometimes made that God must permit us to sin because he can't prevent us from sinning without violating our free will. The Augustinian doctrine of grace teaches, on the contrary, that God not only can prevent every sin but also can restore our will from its bondage to sin so that we freely choose to do what is good. The classic view sees this as an essential feature of Christian eschatology, since in the restoration of all things we will by grace be unable to sin.[19] For when our corruptible selves put on incorruption, the will shall be as free of corruption as the body. We will be as unable to sin as our bodies will be unable to get sick or die, our eyes unable to go blind. Such "inability," if we can even call it that, is not a lack of power or capability but rather the perfection of our capabilities, the fullness of power and freedom, for it delivers us from every evil to which our nature is otherwise vulnerable.[20] Under such a view of grace, there is no kind of evil, not even willful sin, that God must permit in order to preserve the good of free will. Quite the contrary, the grace that makes us permanently incapable of sin is precisely the perfection of our free will and its natural power to love the good.

Thus, in general, there is no kind of good so compelling that it forces God to permit evils. Rather, he freely chooses to permit evils he could have prevented, because in his wisdom he knows how to bring a greater good out of precisely these evils. This means, in effect, that the classic view refuses to let God off the hook. There is a deep sense in which God can be held responsible for every evil, precisely because he freely chose to permit it. That is why, whenever something bad happens, we can ask why. We can ask what reason God could have to let this happen. We might be unable to find an answer,

---

[19]This inability to sin (*non posse peccare*), and why it is the perfection of free will, are topics Augustine treats in the culmination of his great treatise *City of God* 22.30. See also Augustine, *Enchiridion* 28.105.

[20]In very Augustinian fashion Anselm, *Proslogion* 7, points out that the auxiliary verb for "can" or "is able to" (*posse* in Latin, which is etymologically the root of *poder* in Spanish and *pouvoir* in French, as well as *potency* and *possibility* in English) often misleads us by suggesting a kind of power, when in reality the "ability" to sin, suffer, and die is actually an inability or failure to achieve some good. Evil is thus a possibility but never in itself a form of power. This is why there are many things God can't do, which is to say, many inabilities and failures from which he cannot suffer.

but the question itself is never silly or out of bounds. For God does have his reasons, even when they are hidden from us.

HIDDEN REASONS

According to the second part of the greater-good principle, every evil is meaningful in that it serves a good purpose in God's providence. This is what many people find hardest to accept about the classic view. There are, after all, evils so horrendous and destructive that we cannot imagine any good purpose they serve or any good reason for permitting them. There is the torture of children, mass starvation, and genocide, to mention just a few. The classic view would have us trust that God has reasons for allowing such things that are too deep and hidden to be of any comfort to us. It is reasonable to wonder how we can trust that God is good at all if he thinks there is good reason for allowing people to be subjected to afflictions that are so hideous.

Hence a prominent challenge to the classic view in modern theology is to deny that every evil is one God could have prevented, which means denying that every evil is one God permitted. In effect, the aim is to restore trust in God's goodness by getting him off the hook, arguing that his omnipotence is not as extensive and his providence not as meticulous as the classic view teaches. Though he will defeat evil in the end, there are episodes in the middle of the story where we can't see any reasons for our suffering, not because they are hidden but because there are none. In one recent theodicy God is fighting a war against forces of evil that he is sure to win in the long run, but he cannot do so without casualties, including the many people whose particular suffering serves no redeeming purpose.[21] In this view there are a great many evils that are ultimately pointless. The great comfort in such a theodicy is that God hates these evils as much as we do. He hates them too much to permit them, but they happen nonetheless, because he cannot prevent them all. So he shares to some extent in our helplessness in the face of affliction. A good general would love to win the war without any casualties, but in a real war even the best of generals can't accomplish such a thing.

---

[21]Gregory Boyd, *Satan and the Problem of Evil* (Downers Grove, IL: InterVarsity Press, 2001); see esp. 161, 176-77, 371 ("The evil event that happened to us or a loved one may indeed have had no higher purpose"), and 388-89 ("this particular tragedy has no *overarching* reason. . . . She was simply an unfortunate casualty of war").

There are two versions of the classic view—or rather, two implications that I think were mistakenly drawn from it—that do not stand up well against this kind of challenge and have increasingly faded from view in our day. Both of them, I think, fail to reckon fully with the hiddenness of God's reasons for permitting particular evils.

First, there is the notion that because God has his reasons we must accept our suffering. This is to confuse permission with endorsement, as if God's reasons for permitting evil to befall us could not include his intention to help us overcome it. Often this notion is associated with a reading of the Lord's Prayer in which "Thy will be done" means we must resign ourselves to all the evils in our lives as God's will for us. The mistake here is to overlook New Testament eschatology, in which the key movement is not our going to heaven but the kingdom of heaven coming to earth (like the heavenly Jerusalem descending in Rev 21:2). "Thy kingdom come" is asking God to reign in justice, mercy, and glory on earth, as he already does in heaven. Thus "thy will be done on earth as it is in heaven" is of a piece with the genre of complaint in the Psalms, in which the characteristic prayer is "How long, O Lord?" (e.g., Pss 6:3; 13:1; 90:13; cf. Hab 1:2). To pray the Lord's Prayer is to ask, in effect, how long before the kingdom of God comes to earth with its justice and mercy and an end to affliction. In Pauline terms, it is to groan in longing for the day that the corruptible puts on incorruption. The classic view has ample room for such groaning and complaint, though not all of its advocates have seen this. Precisely because it is never silly to ask what God's reasons are for permitting the evils that afflict us, it is also never silly to ask why he does not put a stop to them sooner rather than later. The question might not get an answer, but that is no reason to stop asking, as Jesus' own parable about persistence in prayer illustrates (Lk 18:1-8).

Second, there is a very old habit in the Christian tradition of assuming that suffering and disaster are always a form of punishment or a warning of worse punishment to come. This assumption is based on a reading of the story from Adam to Christ that sees the children of Adam as always guilty and therefore never suffering as innocents. It can draw on large swaths of biblical discourse that speak of the wrath of God, predicting disasters or interpreting disasters that have happened as divine punishment.[22] Any

---

[22]It should not have to be said—but unfortunately it does—that such discourse is found not only in the Old Testament. It is vividly exemplified in the New Testament apocalypses, including not only the book of Revelation but also the "synoptic apocalypse," the long speech Jesus gives a few days before his crucifixion (Mt 24; Mk 13; Lk 21).

theology that takes the Bible seriously will have a place for such discourse. Yet it is not the whole story, and it is surely a mistake to assume that the only good God brings out of the evils that afflict us is the justice of punishment. In Paul's telling of the story, as we have already seen, the whole creation was subjected to futility *in hope,* and the hope is not for more punishment but for liberation from the bondage of corruption and for the glorious freedom of the children of God.

THE SHAPE OF THE STORY

The whole story from Adam to Christ includes both punishment and hope. And as the classic view has always insisted, a proper telling of the story must also include a sober warning to us sinners of the wrath to come, confronting us with the truth that we have a divine judge who is not as persuaded of our innocence as most of us would like to believe. This is a very unpopular truth in the comfortable, affluent lands of the West today, which is why it is all the more important that it continue to be heard. But it will be heard more clearly if it is properly accompanied by Christian hope, which is not just for forgiveness of sins but for a liberation from horrendous evils that seem out of proportion to any guilt we can see in humanity.

The book of Job is of course a key biblical witness on this point. Job insists that it will not do to say that the only meaning of his suffering is punishment. Yet it seems—unlike Paul, for example—that he has no alternative interpretation to offer and no hope for anything better. He complains that God treats him like an enemy, and in the first of his long speeches, in Job 3, all he wants is not to exist. Yet by the middle of the book his complaint takes a singularly bold form: he wishes there were someone in heaven who could arbitrate between himself and God, so that he could be vindicated in heaven itself (Job 9:32-33; 16:19-21; 23:3-7). What Job does not realize is that he already has exactly what he is longing for. There is one who has already vindicated him in heaven; it is God himself, who began the whole story by praising Job for his blamelessness and uprightness (Job 1:8). In fact Job suffers precisely in order to vindicate God's vindication of Job, to show Satan that Job does indeed serve God for nothing (Job 1:9), with no hope of reward. Even Job's complaints, his inability—despite his initial efforts— to give up expecting and even demanding that God show himself to be just, are ways that Job serves and honors God. Instead of trying to justify God, making excuses for him or getting him off the hook, Job cannot let go of the expectation that God should be the just God that Job knows he is.[23]

So the irony is that Job already has what he wants, and that this is precisely why he suffers. For it is essential to the depth of his suffering that he does not know its meaning. He cannot see what good God could possibly bring out of this, and he surely cannot see that the good he clamors for is one he already has. And indeed even at the end of the book he does not find out. I have to wonder whether, with his goods and children restored (following the old rabbinic interpretation that suggests that the children he receives at the end of the story are his dead children resurrected), Job might have laughed if he found out why he actually suffered. At any rate, I do think it is one of the many lessons of the book of Job that the story of our suffering is ultimately comic rather than tragic. As the title of one of Shakespeare's comedies puts it: all's well that ends well. It is not a trivial point. In a comedy the happy ending often changes the meaning of what happens in the middle of the story, and we see that with a laugh, as if to say: "Oh, so *that's* what was really happening—if I had only known!"

The classic view of the world sees the history of the world from Adam's fall to Christ's return as, in a very broad sense, a comedy. It is a story with a happy ending that changes the meaning of all that went before, just as Easter changes the meaning of Good Friday. What we in our present suffering feel as defeat is actually a glorious victory, if we only knew it. But right now we don't know it. Often we are as ignorant of the meaning of our suffering as Job, and this is essential to the meaning of our suffering. Yet the Christian story, which is to say the gospel of Christ, does not let us suffer without hope. For in the light of the gospel we know, as the refrain in a memorable Good Friday sermon once put it, "It's Friday, but Sunday's comin'."[24] We therefore know something of the structure of our hope—that there really is a greater good that comes out of the sufferings of this present

---

[23]On this point, see the interpretation of the book of Job by Karl Barth, *Church Dogmatics* (Edinburgh: T&T Clark, 1961), IV/3.1, in the small print sections, 383-88, 398-408, 421-34. The point that Job's suffering vindicates God's vindication of Job is one I explore from a pastoral perspective in *Good News for Anxious Christians* (Grand Rapids: Brazos, 2010), chap. 8.

[24]For the story of this sermon, see Anthony Campolo, *It's Friday, but Sunday's Comin'* (Waco, TX: Word, 1984), chap. 7.

time—and we know some crucial details about the end of the story, for they are what we are waiting to see when we pray "Thy Kingdom come."

IVAN'S TORTURED CHILDREN

The greater-good principle should therefore not be abandoned in the face of the challenges of modern theodicy. It should instead be reiterated and reaffirmed, with renewed attention to the hiddenness of the greater good that God will bring out of particular evils, since that hiddenness is also essential to the meaning of our suffering.

The point of the reaffirmation can be illustrated in response to one of the great modern statements of the problem of evil, the chapter of Fyodor Dostoevsky's novel *The Brothers Karamazov* in which Ivan Karamazov presents anecdotes from his collection of articles about tortured children.[25] Dostoevsky says in a letter that these were not stories he invented but reports of the torments of real children. The chapter is titled "Rebellion" because Ivan is not doing anything so flatfooted as arguing that God does not exist. He is rebelling against a God he assumes exists. He looks forward to an unimaginable harmony in the future, beyond the grasp of his "pitiful, earthly, Euclidean understanding," as he calls it, in which all suffering will be healed and made up for, all humanity redeemed and reconciled, and we will see "the victim rise up and embrace his murderer . . . when everyone suddenly understands what it has all been for." But it is not a harmony he can accept, because it is "not worth the tears of . . . one tortured child." His rebellion is that "I don't want the harmony. From love of humanity, I don't want it." The price is too high: if the torture of even one child is the price we must pay to enter into this ultimate reconciliation and understanding, then Ivan refuses to pay the price of the entrance ticket: "It's not God that I don't accept . . . only I most respectfully return Him the ticket."[26]

With Dostoevsky himself, who was one of the greatest Christian writers of all time, we ought to say resolutely that Ivan is wrong. "From

---

[25]Fyodor Dostoevsky, *The Brothers Karamazov* (New York: W. W. Norton, 1976), book 5, chap. 4. This Norton critical edition includes a letter dated January 30, 1879, in which Dostoevsky says, "All the anecdotes about children . . . were published in the press. . . . I invented nothing" (758), as well as a selection from Dostoevsky's *Writer's Diary*, February 1976, that describes a trial that was the source of one of Ivan's anecdotes (770-74).

[26]Dostoevsky, *Brothers Karamazov*, 224-26.

love of humanity" he ought not to return the ticket but rather hope to join the tortured child who is reconciled to her own history and her own life. For if the harmony he speaks of does come, then surely she with all creation will praise and thank God with sincere joy for all he is and does, including for the life he gave her. It is indeed unimaginable to our "Euclidean understanding" how this could ever be true—it is like trying to picture parallel lines meeting in the end. We do not have knowledge or access to a greater good that would justify permitting the torture of a child. But if God is as Christian hope says he is, one who is truly worthy of the praise of all creatures, then there are reasons, however unimaginable to us, why every sufferer in this life, including every tortured child, can confess in the end—when all things are restored and we do understand—that God has given her a good life.[27] Hence what we should not let Ivan get away with is the claim that he must turn in the ticket "from love of humanity." Precisely by refusing to accept the hope of reconciliation, Ivan separates himself from hope for the tortured child, from her vindication as well as her healing and restoration.

FELIX CULPA

Dostoevsky's own answer to Ivan, presented obliquely in the next part of *The Brothers Karamazov*, containing the life and reminiscences of the Russian monk Father Zosima, makes claims that go further than the classic view.[28] If we loved all God's creatures, Zosima says, we would perceive the divine mystery in things and find that "life is a paradise" that already "lies hidden within all of us."[29] The classic view is less mystical and more eschatological than this. The great mystery is hidden not within us but in Christ at God's right hand, where our life too is hidden until he is revealed in glory (Col 3:3-4). Paradise and perfection are not yet here, but we await their coming from above, where Christ is. Thus the medieval visionary Julian of Norwich articulates the classic view when she writes of Christ speaking in the future

---

[27]This is my way of stating the central point in Marilyn Adams's important book *Horrendous Evils and the Goodness of God* (Ithaca, NY: Cornell University Press, 1999).

[28]In several letters, Dostoevsky explicitly says this part of the novel is an answer to Ivan, though an oblique one; Dostoevsky, *Brothers Karamazov*, 757, 761-62.

[29]Ibid., 282. Cf. 298.

tense: "I shall make all things well, and I will make all things well; and you will see yourself that every kind of thing will be well."[30]

Christian hope locates us in an eschatology, which is to say in a story that has an ending (an *eschaton* in Greek), which like the happy ending in many a good story reveals the greater good that makes sense of the suffering and evil in the middle of the story. But as in many comedies, the middle of the story can be dark and grotesque, and no fun at all for the people in it—like the central acts of *A Midsummer Night's Dream* when the four lovers lost in the woods seem to have gone crazy, forgetting who they are and who is their true love. Characters in the midst of such a comedy are in no position to laugh. They are not in paradise, and they must hope this night will come to an end.

One way to state the problem of evil in its pastoral dimension is to ask, like the characters in such a comedy: what reason do we have to think that the story we're living in really is a good story, one with a happy ending that makes sense of the dark and grotesque things that happen in the middle? This leads to the very serious theological question: What reason do we have to trust that a God who is providentially sovereign over *this* story, the one we actually live in, really is good—and not just in the abstract, but good *for us*?

The way the Augustinian tradition gets at this question is to ask what greater good God intends to bring out of Adam's sin and all the evils that follow from it. As always, the assumption is that these are evils God could have prevented. This means God chose for us a story in which we are sinners, justly punished in many ways for and by the consequences of our own sins, but also redeemed by the suffering of his own Son, who is God in the flesh. There is a striking and famous moment in the liturgy of the Western church that affirms the goodness of this choice, seeing in the glory of Christ's resurrection, with all that follows from it, the greater good that is the reason why God did not prevent Adam's sin. It takes place on the Easter Vigil, in the *Exsultet*, which is the prayer sung or recited at the lighting of the Paschal candle, representing that moment in the dark night before Sunday morning when, with no human eye to see it, Christ's resurrection took place. Gathered around the lit candle, the church thanks God for being part of this story in

---

[30]Julian of Norwich, *Showings* (New York: Paulist, 1978), 229; from the "Long Text" of her work, more commonly known under the title *A Revelation of Love*, chap. 31.

famous words that declare Adam's sin to be a happy fault (*felix culpa*) because it required Christ to come to undo it.

Two verses in particular are worth looking at closely:

O surely necessary sin of Adam, which was destroyed by Christ's death!
O happy fault, that deserved to have so great a Redeemer![31]

The notion is not that Adam's sin was necessary in the abstract, as if it had to happen. Rather, it was necessary if we were to have so great a Redeemer, God in the flesh suffering with us and for us and defeating death itself on this night. God is praised for this, because he could have chosen otherwise. Because Adam's sin was not necessary in the abstract, the world need not have been a story of sin and redemption. God could have created a good world and allowed no moral evil in it, but then there could have been no Christ crucified and raised from the dead. Instead, God freely chose to create a world with a more difficult and more beautiful story, in which there is both Adam and Christ, sin and redemption, Good Friday and Easter Sunday, as well as the movement from the one to the other.

The conceptual point is that while evil in general is not necessary for the good, there are certain kinds of good that cannot exist without certain kinds of evil, precisely because they are goods that defeat specific evils, as Christ's death destroys the whole legacy of Adam's sin. If the world is to be the eschatological story told in the New Testament, then it will have to have something like Adam's sin (and again, there are differences within the Augustinian tradition as to how literally to take the story in Genesis). The point is that the world did not have to be such a story. It could have been a simpler and easier story, with no sinners and therefore no Redeemer. But God freely chose that it be *this* story, the one we actually live in, which the Scripture calls the gospel of Christ. And on the night of Christ's resurrection, the church praises and thanks God that this is the story of the world in which we live.

But that is only one night of the year. On other nights the church has other things to say. Far more often over the course of the year it is praying

---

[31]The words are so bold and striking that it is best to confirm them by giving the original Latin:
O certe necessarium Adae peccatum, quod Christi morte deletum est!
O felix culpa, quae talem ac tantum meruit habere Redemptorem!

Psalms with the words "How long?" For we cannot simply stay happy that we are in a good story. It is a good story because it has a glorious, happy ending, which we have not reached yet. Nor have the tortured children. We do not know, in any detail, how the redemption that is in Christ can be so great a good that it will make sense of their suffering and allow them to praise God sincerely and joyously for the life he has given them. So the church cannot stay long at the Easter Vigil. The liturgy moves on in time, from Good Friday to Easter Sunday and beyond, to the hope for Christ's return that is prominent in the season of Advent, thus opening the cycle of the liturgical year to the future. So in liturgical prayer we do not treat every day as if it were the same, but we move forward in the story of Christ, inhabiting the gospel, which enfolds our lives from past to future.

In the *Exsultet* we give thanks repeatedly for what happened "on this night," identifying ourselves in terms of a past that looks forward to our future, and in the season of Advent we remember the first coming of Christ as we await his second coming, in hymns such as "O Come, O Come, Emmanuel." The church must continue to await actively the coming of the Lord's kingdom, which means among other things doing what it can to put an end to the torture of children. Yet in its necessary activism it must not neglect the work of liturgy, which is the practical work that most deeply gives shape to our hope—praying without ceasing, not only "How long?" but also "Thy Kingdom come." The best reasons I can think of for trusting that God is good are most fully available to those who participate in this life of the body of Christ in liturgical time, which comes back once a year to the night when we can say that Adam's sin was a happy fault, because it required so great a Redeemer.

2

A Molinist View

WILLIAM LANE CRAIG

In Frank Capra's movie *It's a Wonderful Life*, the angel sent by God to George Bailey reveals to him what the world would have been like had he never been born. To his shock, he finds the world dramatically changed. Had seemingly minor events in his life never occurred, dramatic and far-reaching effects would have ensued, transforming the lives of others far beyond his seemingly quiet and mundane life in Bedford Falls. What the angel mediates to George Bailey is the truth of various subjunctive conditional (or counterfactual) propositions concerning his life, and the film illustrates the sweeping and unforeseeable differences that the actualization of the antecedents of such counterfactuals can make.

MOLINISM

God's knowledge of such counterfactuals logically prior to his creation of the world lay at the heart of Counter-Reformation theologian Luis Molina's theory of providence. Logically prior to his decree to create the world, God possesses not only knowledge of everything that free creatures *could* do (natural knowledge) but also of everything that they *would* do in any appropriately specified set of circumstances (middle knowledge).

God's natural knowledge gives him knowledge of all necessary truths. By means of it God knows what is the full range of possible worlds. He knows, for example, that in some possible world in a certain set of circumstances Peter freely denies Christ three times and that in another world Peter freely affirms Christ under identical circumstances, for both are possible.

God's middle knowledge gives him knowledge of all true counterfactual propositions of creaturely freedom. For example, logically prior to his creative decree, God knew that *if Peter were in circumstances C, he would freely deny Christ three times*. These counterfactuals serve to delimit the range of possible worlds to worlds that are feasible for God to actualize. For example, there is a possible world in which Peter freely affirms Christ in precisely the same circumstances in which he in fact denied him; but given the counterfactual truth that if Peter were in precisely those circumstances he would freely deny Christ, then the possible world in which Peter freely affirms Christ in those circumstances is not feasible for God. God could *make* Peter affirm Christ in those circumstances, but then his confession would not be free.

By means of his middle knowledge, God knows what is the proper subset of possible worlds that are feasible for him, given the counterfactuals that are true. God then decrees to create certain free creatures in certain circumstances and simultaneously decides how he himself would freely act in any circumstances, thus giving him knowledge of counterfactuals of divine freedom. On the basis of his middle knowledge and his knowledge of his own decree, God then has complete knowledge of the actual world (free knowledge), including foreknowledge of everything that *will* happen.

Only the content of God's free knowledge depends on God's will. The content of his natural knowledge and of his middle knowledge is, so to speak, prevolitional and therefore independent of his will. We can vividly illustrate the stages of God's knowledge by imagining him being dealt a hand of cards. First, he is dealt a hand having all the necessary truths printed on them. God is thus not at liberty to actualize contradictory states of affairs, for they are not in the cards. Next, he is dealt a hand of cards having all true counterfactuals of creaturely freedom printed on them. Although these truths, unlike necessary truths, are contingent, nevertheless they are prevolitional for God, in that he does not decide what creatures would freely do in various circumstances.

God must now play with the hand he has been dealt, that is to say, actualize a world that is feasible for him given the counterfactuals that are true. If we imagine God existing in various possible worlds, in some possible worlds he might have been dealt a very lousy hand indeed. The Reformed theologian might imagine God, surveying the range of feasible worlds, deciding that none of the worlds containing libertarian free creatures is worth actualizing and therefore deciding to actualize a world in which he himself determines everything that happens! Molina, on the other hand, thought that God has decided to actualize a world of libertarian free creatures and to skillfully play the hand he has been dealt in such a way that his ultimate ends are achieved through creaturely free decisions, despite the sinful decisions they would make and the evils they would bring about.

Molina's theory of middle knowledge provides the basis for his doctrine of divine providence. Molina defines providence as God's ordering of things to their ends, either directly or mediately through secondary agents. Molina carefully distinguishes between God's absolute intentions and his conditional intentions concerning free creatures. It is, for example, God's absolute intention that no creature should ever sin and that all should reach heaven. But it is not within God's power to determine what decisions creatures would freely take in various circumstances. In certain circumstances, creatures will freely sin, despite the fact that it is God's will that they not sin. If, then, God for whatever reason wants to bring about those circumstances, he has no choice but to allow the creature to sin, even though that is not his absolute intention. God's absolute intentions are thus often frustrated by sinful creatures, but his conditional intentions, which take into account creatures' free actions, are always fulfilled. Even sin serves God's conditional intentions in that it manifests his overflowing goodness in the incarnation of Christ for the purpose of rescuing humanity from sin, his power in his redeeming humanity from sin, and his justice in punishing sin.

God's providence, then, extends to everything that happens, but it does not follow that God wills positively everything that happens. God wills positively every good creaturely decision, but evil decisions he does not will but merely permits. Molina explains,

> All *good* things, whether produced by causes acting from a necessity of nature or by free causes, depend upon divine predetermination . . . and providence in such a way that each is specifically intended by God through His predetermination and providence, whereas the *evil* acts of the created will are subject as well to divine predetermination and providence to the extent that the causes from which they emanate and the general concurrence on God's part required to elicit them are granted through divine predetermination and

providence—though not in order that *these particular acts* should emanate from them, but rather in order that *other, far different, acts* might come to be, and in order that the innate freedom of the things endowed with a will might be preserved for their maximum benefit; in addition evil acts are subject to that same divine predetermination and providence to the extent that they cannot exist in particular unless God by His providence *permits them in particular* in the service of some greater good. It clearly follows from the above that all things without exception are *individually* subject to God's will and providence, which intend certain of them *as particulars* and permit the rest *as particulars.*[1]

Everything that happens, therefore, occurs either by God's will or permission and thus falls under his providence.

THE PROBLEM OF EVIL

What relevance does Molinism have to the problem of evil? That depends on which version of the problem is under discussion. Contemporary philosophers of religion have found it helpful to distinguish between the *intellectual* problem of evil and the *emotional* problem of evil. The intellectual problem of evil concerns how to give a rationally acceptable account of the coexistence of God and evil. The emotional problem of evil concerns how to dissolve the emotional aversion people have to a God who would permit such evil. The intellectual problem lies in the province of the philosopher; the emotional problem lies in the province of the pastor.

Intellectual problem of evil. We can further distinguish significantly different versions of the intellectual problem. Sometimes the distinction is drawn between the deductive or logical version of the problem and the probabilistic or evidential version. It seems to me, however, that these two versions of the problem are best distinguished as the *internal* versus the *external* problem of evil. That is to say, the problem can be presented in terms of premises to which the Christian theist is or ought to be committed as a Christian, so that the Christian worldview is somehow at odds with itself. On the other hand, the problem can be presented in terms of premises to which the Christian theist is not committed as a Christian but that we nonetheless

---

[1]Luis Molina, *On Divine Foreknowledge* 4.53.3.17, trans. Alfred J. Freddoso (Ithaca, NY: Cornell University Press, 1988).

have good reason to regard as true. The first approach tries to expose an inner tension within the Christian worldview itself; the second approach attempts to present evidence against the truth of the Christian worldview.

Internal problem of evil. Now the internal problem of evil again takes two forms: the *logical* version and the *probabilistic* version. In the logical version of the problem, the atheist's goal is to show that it is logically impossible for both God and evil to exist. There is no possible world in which God and evil coexist, any more than there is a possible world in which an irresistible force and an immovable object both exist. The two are logically incompatible. If one exists, the other does not. The Christian worldview (unlike certain types of Hinduism, for example) is committed to the reality of evil, just as it is committed to the reality of an omnipotent and omnibenevolent God. Since evil exists, the argument goes, it follows logically that God must not exist. Thus the Christian worldview embodies an inner contradiction.

In the probabilistic version of the problem, the admission is made that it is possible that God and evil coexist, but it is insisted that it is highly improbable that both God and the evil in the world exist. Thus the Christian theist is committed to two beliefs that tend to undermine each other. Since he believes that the evil in the world is real, he should find it highly improbable that God exists.

LOGICAL VERSION. The logical version of the internal problem of evil holds that the two statements

(1) An omnipotent, omnibenevolent God exists.

and

(2) Evil exists.

are logically incompatible. For centuries this has been the form usually assumed by the problem of evil. Indeed, as late as the mid-twentieth century atheists such as J. L. Mackie propounded the problem in this form.

This version of the problem is resolved quite independently of the resources of Molinism. As Alvin Plantinga has explained, the proponent of the logical version of the problem of evil has assumed an enormous burden of proof that he cannot sustain. For at face value, statements (1) and (2) are not logically inconsistent.[2] There is no explicit contradiction between them.

---

[2]See Alvin Plantinga, *The Nature of Necessity* (Oxford, Clarendon, 1974).

If the atheist thinks that they are implicitly contradictory, then he must be assuming some hidden premises that would serve to bring out the contradiction and make it explicit. But what are those premises?

There seem to be two:

(3) If God is omnipotent, then he can create any world that he desires.

and

(4) If God is omnibenevolent, then he prefers a world without evil over a world with evil.

The atheist reasons that since God is omnipotent, he could create a world containing free creatures who always freely choose to do the right thing. By the same token, being omnipotent, God could as well create such a world free of pain and suffering. Moreover, since God is also omnibenevolent, the objector continues, he would, of course, prefer such a world to any world infected with evil and suffering. Since God both can and would create a world without suffering and evil, it follows from the evil and suffering in the world that God does not exist.

Plantinga points out that both (3) and (4) must be *necessarily* true if the atheist's argument is to succeed in showing that there is no possible world in which God and evil coexist. But the atheist has not shown that these assumptions are necessarily true.

As to (3), if there is a possible world in which creatures have libertarian freedom (even if in fact they do not), then (3) is not necessarily true. For God's being omnipotent does not imply that he can do logical impossibilities, such as make a round square or make someone freely choose to do something. Thus, if God grants people genuine freedom to choose as they like, then it is impossible for him to guarantee what their choices will be. Now what that implies is that if creatures have libertarian freedom, there are possible worlds which God is incapable of actualizing. Such worlds are not feasible for God. Suppose, then, that in some possible world there are no worlds feasible for God in which creatures always freely choose to do the right thing. Thus it is possible that every world feasible for God that contains free creatures is a world with evil.

Moreover, as for suffering apparently due to natural causes, Plantinga points out that this could be the result of demonic activity in the world.

Demons can have freedom just like human beings, and it is possible that God could not preclude natural suffering without removing the free will of demonic creatures. Now one might think that such a resolution to the problem of natural suffering is ridiculous and even frivolous, but that would be to confuse the *logical* problem of evil with the *probabilistic* problem of evil. The atheist needs to show that such an explanation is logically impossible, otherwise his argument that God and evil are logically incompatible fails. But no atheist has been able to prove that, necessarily, an omnipotent God can create any world he desires. Therefore the objector's argument on this ground alone fails.

But what about (4), that if God is omnibenevolent, then he prefers a world without evil over a world with evil? Again, such an assumption has not been shown to be necessarily true. In some possible world God might permit suffering in order to build or to test people or to achieve some other overriding end. Thus, even though God is omnibenevolent, he might well have morally sufficient reasons for permitting evil and suffering in the world. Consequently, the second assumption of our objector, that an omni-benevolent God prefers a world with no evil over a world with evil, is also not necessarily true. The argument thus doubly fails.

Plantinga argues that we can go even further than this. Not only has the atheist failed to prove that God and evil are inconsistent, but we can, on the contrary, prove that they are consistent. In order to do that, all we have to do is provide some possible explanation of the evil in the world that is compatible with God's existence. And the following is such an explanation:

(5) God could not have created a world that had so much good as the actual world but had less evil, both in terms of quantity and quality; and, moreover, God has morally sufficient reasons for permitting the evil that exists.

The "could not" in (5) should be understood to mean that such a world is infeasible for God. There are doubtless logically possible worlds that are sinless and exceed the actual world in goodness, but such worlds might not be feasible for God. So long as this explanation is even possible, it proves that God and the evil in the world are logically compatible.

The atheist could insist that perhaps (1) and (5) are, after all, logically incompatible in some way we cannot discern. Perhaps in every possible world in which God exists the counterfactuals of creaturely freedom that are true in that world permit him to create a world having more good but less evil than the actual world. But this point is of little significance. For it is the atheist who bears the burden of proof to show that there is no possible world in which (1) and (2) are true, because it is the atheist who claims to have discerned a contradiction within a Christian worldview. That is an enormously heavy burden that has proved to be unbearable. After centuries of discussion, contemporary philosophers, including most atheists and agnostics, have come to recognize this fact. It is now widely admitted that the logical problem of evil is a failure.

Thus Molinism is of little direct relevance to the logical version of the internal problem of evil. That version founders on the unbearable burden of proof it places on the atheist's shoulders.

PROBABILISTIC VERSION. Rather, Molinism's relevance will become evident when it comes to the probabilistic version of the internal problem. Here the atheist claims that the evil and suffering in the world make it highly improbable, if not impossible, that God exists. The Christian theist can offer a many-faceted response to this claim.

1. *Relative to the full scope of the evidence, God's existence is probable.* If the logical version of the internal problem of evil were a sound argument, then God would not exist, case closed. But probabilities are relative to one's background information. Thus, with a probability argument, we have to ask: *Probable with respect to what?* The atheist claims that God's existence is improbable. But with respect to what? To the evil in the world? If that is all the background information one considers, then it is hardly surprising if God's existence should appear improbable relative to that alone. But the Christian theist will insist that we consider not just the evil in the world but all the evidence relevant to God's existence. When we take into account the full scope of the evidence, the Christian theist might maintain, then the existence of God becomes quite probable. Hence the theist could actually admit that the problem of evil, taken in isolation, does make God's existence improbable. But he will insist that when the total scope of the evidence is considered, then the scales are at least evenly balanced or tip in favor of theism.

Indeed, the theist might insist that insofar as the probabilistic problem of evil is taken to be an internal problem for the theist, there is nothing whatsoever objectionable or irrational in believing statements that are improbable with respect to each other, so long as one knows them both to be true. For example, relative to the background information of human reproductive biology, one's own personal existence is astronomically improbable. Yet there is nothing irrational about believing both the facts of human reproductive biology and that one exists. Similarly, if one is warranted in believing that God exists, then there is no problem occasioned by the fact that this belief is improbable relative to the evil in the world.

2. *We are not in a good position to assess with confidence the probability that God lacks morally sufficient reasons for permitting the evils that occur.* Whether God's existence is improbable relative to the evil in the world depends on how probable it is that God has morally sufficient reasons for permitting the evils that occur. It is at this point that Molinism becomes so relevant to the problem of evil. For a God endowed with middle knowledge can have morally sufficient reasons for permitting events that far transcend the foresight of any temporally bound person not so endowed. A person who lacks middle knowledge will be unable to assess the long-term consequences of the events that he permits to happen and so cannot have reasons for permitting them that are indiscernible from the standpoint of the present.

By contrast, the transcendent and sovereign God of Molinism sees the end of history from its beginning and providentially orders history so that his purposes are ultimately achieved through free decisions by humans. In order to achieve his ends God might well have to permit certain evils along the way. Evils that appear pointless or unnecessary to us within our limited framework might be seen to have been justly permitted within God's wider framework. The brutal murder of an innocent man or a child's dying of leukemia could send a ripple effect through history such that God's morally sufficient reason for permitting it might not emerge until centuries later or perhaps in another country. Being limited in space and time, in intelligence and insight, we are simply in no epistemic position to make probability judgments to the effect that "God probably does not have a morally sufficient reason for permitting this event to occur" with any sort of confidence.

Already in nineteenth-century classical physics, it was appreciated that the existence of what James Clerk Maxwell called "singular points" makes it impossible to predict the outcome of present, visible causes:

For example, the rock loosed by frost and balanced on a singular point of the mountain-side, the little spark which kindles the great forest, the little word which sets the world a-fighting, the little scruple which prevents a man from doing his will, the little spore which blights all the potatoes, the little gemmule which makes us philosophers or idiots. Every existence above a certain rank has its singular points: the higher the rank, the more of them. At these points, influences whose physical magnitude is too small to be taken account of by a finite being, may produce results of the greatest importance.[3]

Similarly, in the developing field of chaos theory, scientists have discovered that certain macroscopic systems, for example, weather systems or insect populations, are extraordinarily sensitive to the tiniest perturbations. A butterfly fluttering on a branch in West Africa might set in motion forces that would eventually issue in a hurricane over the Atlantic Ocean. Yet it is impossible in principle for anyone observing that butterfly palpitating on a branch to predict such an outcome.

Only an omniscient mind endowed with middle knowledge could grasp the complexities involved in directing a world of free creatures toward one's previsioned goals. One has only to think of the innumerable, incalculable contingencies involved in arriving at a single historical event, say, the Allied victory at D-day. We have no idea of the natural and moral evils that might be involved in order for God to arrange the circumstances and free agents in them requisite to some intended purpose, nor can we discern what reasons such a provident God might have in mind for permitting some evil to enter our lives. Certainly many evils seem pointless and unnecessary to us—but we are simply not in a position to judge.

To say this is not to appeal to mystery but rather to point to the inherent cognitive limitations that frustrate attempts to say that it is improbable that a God endowed with middle knowledge has a morally sufficient reason for permitting some particular evil. We might be able to blame a God who shares similar limitations to ours for not intervening to stop the evils once they start to unfold, but we are in no position to make such a claim about a God endowed with middle knowledge.

---

[3]J. C. Maxwell, "On Science and Free Will," in *The Scientific Letters and Papers of James Clerk Maxwell*, vol. 2, *1862–1873*, ed. P. M. Harman (Cambridge: Cambridge University Press, 1995), 822.

Ironically, in other contexts nonbelievers recognize the problems posed by these cognitive limitations. One of the most damaging objections to utilitarian ethical theory, for example, is that it is quite simply impossible for us to estimate which action that we might perform will ultimately lead to the greatest amount of happiness or pleasure in the world. Because of our cognitive limitations, actions that appear disastrous in the short term might redound to the greatest good, while some short-term boon might issue in untold misery. Once we contemplate God's providence over the whole of history, then it becomes evident how hopeless it is for limited observers to speculate on the probability of God's having morally sufficient reasons for the evils that we see. We are simply not in a good position to assess such probabilities with any confidence.

3. *Christian theism entails doctrines that increase the probability of the coexistence of God and evil.* The objector maintains that if God exists, then it is improbable that the world would contain the evil it does. Now what the Christian can do in response to such an assertion is to offer various hypotheses that would tend to raise the probability of evil given God's existence: Pr (Evil|God&Hypotheses) > Pr (Evil|God). He can appeal to certain key Christian doctrines in order to show that evil is not so improbable on Christian theism as on some bare-boned theism. For example, he might appeal to the following hypotheses:

The chief purpose of life is not happiness but the knowledge of God.

Humankind is in a state of rebellion against God and his purpose.

God's purpose is not restricted to this life but spills over beyond the grave into eternal life.

The knowledge of God is an incommensurable good.

Given such doctrines, it seems that evil is not so improbable after all. Thus it turns out that answering the probabilistic problem of evil is easier from the Christian perspective than from the perspective of mere theism. Since the problem is being presented as an internal problem for the Christian theist, there is nothing illicit about the Christian theist's availing himself of all the resources of his worldview in answering the objection.

Molinism is especially relevant to the explication of the first doctrine above. One reason that the problem of evil seems so intractable is that people tend naturally to assume that if God exists, then his purpose for human life is happiness in this world. God's role is to provide a comfortable environment for his human pets. But on the Christian view, this is false. We are not God's pets, and the goal of human life is not happiness per se but the knowledge of God—which in the end will bring true and everlasting human fulfillment. Many evils occur in life that might be utterly pointless with respect to the goal of producing human happiness; but they might not be pointless with respect to producing a deeper knowledge of God.

Because God's ultimate goal for humanity is the knowledge of himself—which alone can bring eternal happiness to creatures—history cannot be seen in its true perspective apart from considerations pertinent to the kingdom of God. British divine Martyn Lloyd-Jones writes,

> The key to the history of the world is the kingdom of God. . . . From the very beginning, . . . God has been at work establishing a new kingdom in the world. It is His own kingdom, and He is calling people out of the world into that kingdom: and everything that happens in the world has relevance to it. . . . Other events are of importance as they have a bearing upon that event. The problems of today are to be understood only in its light. . . .
>
> Let us not therefore be stumbled when we see surprising things happening in the world. Rather let us ask, "What is the relevance of this event to the kingdom of God?" Or, if strange things are happening to you personally, don't complain but say, "What is God teaching me through this?" . . . We need not become bewildered and doubt the love or the justice of God. . . . We should . . . judge every event in the light of God's great, eternal and glorious purpose.[4]

Here Molinism has an important role to play. It might well be the case that natural and moral evils are part of the means God uses to draw people into his kingdom. This is not some airy-fairy speculation but is borne out by contemporary demographics. A reading of a missions handbook such as *Operation World* reveals that it is precisely in countries that have endured severe hardship that evangelical Christianity is growing at its greatest rates, while growth curves in the indulgent West are nearly flat. Consider, for example, the following reports:[5]

---

[4]Martyn Lloyd-Jones, *From Fear to Faith* (London: Inter-Varsity Press, 1953), 23-24.
[5]Patrick Johnstone, *Operation World* (Grand Rapids: Zondervan, 1993), 164, 207-8, 214; Jason Mandryk, *Operation World*, 7th ed. (Colorado Springs: Biblica, 2010), 393-94, 610, 611, 613.

China:

It is estimated that 20 million Chinese lost their lives during Mao's Cultural Revolution. Christians stood firm in what was probably the most widespread and harsh persecution the Church has ever experienced. The persecution purified and indigenized the Church. Since 1977 the growth of the Church in China has no parallels in history. Researchers estimate that there were 30-75 million Christians by 1990. Mao Zedong unwittingly became the greatest evangelist in history.

El-Salvador:

The 12-year civil war, earthquakes, and the collapse of the price of coffee, the nation's main export, impoverished the nation. Over 80% live in dire poverty. An astonishing spiritual harvest has been gathered from all strata of society in the midst of the hate and bitterness of war. In 1960 evangelicals were 2.3% of the population, but today are around 20%.

Ethiopia:

Ethiopia is in a state of shock. Her population struggles with the trauma of millions of deaths through repression, famine, and war. Two great waves of violent persecution refined and purified the Church, but there were many martyrs. There have been millions coming to Christ. Protestants were fewer than 0.8% of the population in 1960, but by 1990 this may have become 13% of the population.

Myanmar:

The military junta has redefined the term "ruthless." A policy of systematic violence against certain minorities yields a harvest of destroyed villages, rape, torture, uprooted populations and international condemnation. The currency is devaluing, food and fuel prices are rising quickly, and people live from hand to mouth with a little to spare—10% are chronically malnourished. The military regime seeks to destroy Christianity (which it calls "the C-virus"), yet faith keeps spreading. Adversity, persecution and isolation have helped shape a resilient, enduring faith. When [the cyclone Nargis] ripped through the country in May 2008, around 140,000 people lost their lives from the storm itself and the disease and deprivation that followed. The aftermath of cyclone Nargis, while tragic, created an open door for the practical ministry of providing food, water, clothing, shelter, and other basic necessities, as well as meeting the deeper economic, spiritual, and psychological needs of the survivors. The response by many Christians and the openness of many Buddhists led to the cyclone being referred to as "the blessed storm." The continued growth of the church amid great suffering and repression is an answer to prayer. Praise God for the refining of the Church, made possible by the desperation of persecution, poverty, and isolation. Liberal groups are drawn closer to biblical truth, and lax believers are driven toward a more dynamic life of faith. Myanmar is a classic example of how suffering, while lamentable, serves to accomplish God's purposes for His people.

Haiti:
The earthquake of 2010 was a disaster on many levels. But it also offers hope out of tragedy. It is believed that 230,000 lost their lives, 300,000 were injured, and over one million were rendered homeless. The spiritual response to the tragedy of the 2010 earthquake was an almost universal outpouring of prayer, repentance, and calling upon God for mercy and deliverance. Out of the disaster God appears to be doing something radical and new among the people of Haiti. Seth Barnes (Adventures in Missions) reports: "Something remarkable is happening over there. It's unprecedented in my experience as a missionary. . . . 'Revival' is too small a word for what we saw in Haiti. Often we weren't able to move our vehicles because of the parades of people praising Jesus' name, carrying placards saying, 'Jesus is Lord.' And everywhere there were prayer meetings—groups as small as 20 or as large as 60,000. . . . Three months ago the pastors of Haiti . . . prayed for revival. They prayed that God would shake their land. They prayed that He would tear down the strongholds. . . . The spiritual atmosphere of the country is completely different now. Voodoo priests by the hundreds have given their lives to Christ."[6]

Moral and natural evils might serve a redemptive purpose in God's plan for a fallen humanity. I think it not at all improbable that only in a world suffused with natural and moral evils would a significant percentage of the world's population freely come to know God and find eternal life.

The history of humankind has been a history of suffering and war. Yet it has also been a history of the advance of the kingdom of God. Figure 1 is a chart released in 1990 by the US Center for World Mission documenting the growth in evangelical Christianity over the centuries. (Neither category includes merely nominal Christians. Even if all of these were included with the non-Christians, there would still today be only about nine nonbelievers for every evangelical believer in the world.)

---

[6]The report by Seth Barnes was received by our missions committee at Johnson Ferry Baptist Church.

THE DIMINISHING TASK

Across the centuries, the constantly decreasing number of
non-Christians per **committed Christian**.

Non-Christian here means "people who do not
consider themselves to be Christians."

Committed Christians here means people
who read, believe and obey the Bible.

The **specific numbers** here
are correct within a small
percentage, except for
the earlier centuries.

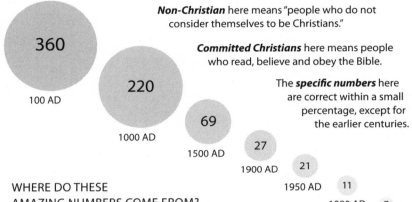

360
100 AD

220
1000 AD

69
1500 AD

27
1900 AD

21
1950 AD

11
1980 AD

7
1989 AD

WHERE DO THESE
AMAZING NUMBERS COME FROM?

They were arrived at by the various contributors to the
Lausanne Statistics Task Force, headed by David Barrett, PhD,
who is the author of the *World Christian Encyclopedia*. The specific figures
are in the table below. The numbers in the column on the right are those used
in this diagram.

These are the numbers in the diagram above. Despite the rapid increase of world population,
Christianity is simply growing faster than any other global religion when what is measured is
its most relevant type of growth—the growth of committed adherents.

Column 1 DATE	Column 2 Non-Christians	Column 3 Com. Christians	Astounding Trend
100 AD	180	0.5	360
1000 AD	220	1	220
1500 AD	344	5	69
1900 AD	1,062	40	27
1950 AD	1,650	80	21
1980 AD	3,025	275	11
1989 AD	3,438	500	7
	The above numbers are published by the Lausanne Statistics Task Force. Note: figures in these two columns are millions		(Column 2 divided by Column 3)

Figure 1. Ratio of non-Christians to committed Christians over history. Chart adapted from *Mission Frontiers*,
November 1990, missionfrontiers.org. Reprinted with permission.

According to Patrick Johnstone, "We are living in the time of the largest ingathering of people into the Kingdom of God that the world has ever seen."[7] It is not at all improbable that this astonishing growth in God's kingdom is due in part to the presence of natural and moral evils in the world. Only a God endowed with middle knowledge could so providentially order the world that through these evils people would come freely into God's kingdom.

Taken together, these considerations make it not improbable that God and the evil in the world should both exist. Middle knowledge will facilitate the providential ordering of a world of free creatures such that evils are justly permitted by God.

External problem of evil. The versions of the problem of evil thus far discussed have tried to show that two beliefs held by Christians, namely, that God exists and that the world contains the evils that we observe, are either inconsistent or improbable with respect to each other. Most nontheists have now abandoned that project. Instead they claim that the apparently pointless and unnecessary evils in the world constitute *evidence* against God's existence. That is to say, they argue that

(6) An omnipotent, omnibenevolent God exists.

and

(7) Gratuitous evil exists.

are incompatible with each other. What makes this an external problem is that the Christian is not committed by his worldview to admitting the truth of (7). The Christian is committed to the truth that *evil exists* but not that *gratuitous evil exists.* The objector is therefore presenting an argument against (Christian) theism of the form

(8) If God exists, gratuitous evil does not exist.

(9) Gratuitous evil exists.

(10) Therefore, God does not exist.

---

[7]Johnstone, *Operation World*, 25. According to the current edition of *Operation World*, evangelical Christianity is growing faster than any other world religion or global religious movement. Evangelicals numbered 89 million, or 2.9 percent, of the world's population in 1960; by 2010 there were 546 million, or 7.9 percent (Mandryk, *Operation World*, 6).

The key question will be the warrant offered for (9). The theist will readily admit that much of the evil we observe in the world appears to be pointless and unnecessary and, hence, gratuitous. But he might challenge the objector's inference from the appearance of gratuitous evil to the reality of gratuitous evil. Here again Molinism will be relevant to the external problem, in the same way that it was relevant to the probabilistic internal problem of evil. The atheist objector must assume that if we do not discern God's morally sufficient reasons for allowing certain evils to occur, then it is probable that there is no such reason—that is to say, that such evils are gratuitous. But we have already seen how uncertain and tenuous such probability judgments on our part are. Our failure to discern the morally justifying reason for the occurrence of various evils gives very little ground for thinking that a God endowed with middle knowledge could not have morally sufficient reasons for permitting the evils we observe in the world.

We should also note that premise (8) itself is not obviously true. Some theists have suggested that while God could eliminate this or that specific evil without decreasing the goodness of the world, nevertheless there must exist a certain amount of gratuitous evil in the world if the goodness of the world is not to be impaired. Thus the probability that a certain specified evil is gratuitous would not adversely affect theism.

Considerations pertinent to divine middle knowledge also arise at this point. It is epistemically possible that only in a world in which gratuitous natural and moral evils exist that the relevant counterfactuals of creaturely freedom are true to enable God to bring the optimal number of persons freely to salvation and the knowledge of himself. The atheist might say that in that case the evils are not really gratuitous after all: they serve the greater good of securing people's eternal salvation. But if one allows a greater good of that sort to count against the gratuity of some evil, then that makes it all the more difficult for the atheist to prove that truly gratuitous evil exists, for how could he possibly surmise what in God's providential plan for history does or does not contribute to the ultimate salvation of the greatest number of people?

Emotional problem of evil. The intellectual problem of evil—whether in its internal or external versions—can thus be satisfactorily solved, and Molinism will make the task easier. But, of course, when one says "solved" one means "philosophically solved." All these mental machinations might be of little comfort to someone who is intensely suffering from some undeserved evil in life. This leads us to the second aspect of the problem mentioned earlier: the emotional problem of evil.

For many people the problem of evil is not really an intellectual problem: it is an emotional problem. They are hurting inside and perhaps bitter against a God who would permit them or others to suffer so. Never mind that there are philosophical solutions to the problem of evil—they do not care and simply reject a God who allows such suffering as we find in the world.

I think that Molinism can be of emotional comfort to people who are suffering from the emotional problem of evil. (At least it is to me!) Some open theists report that certain people find genuine comfort in the thought that God is not providentially in control of the world and so cannot be held responsible for planning the evils that have befallen them. I can understand why some people would be comforted by the thought that there is a cognitively limited Superman on their side who is aligned with them in the struggle against evil and suffering and who cannot be blamed for the bad things that he did not see coming. But I wonder if such people have really thought through the open theist alternative. It doesn't take a genius to see that certain terrible moral or natural evils are about to happen, and a cognitively limited Superman would often seem blameworthy for not preventing or stopping them. Evils that appear to be gratuitous are much more likely to actually be so, absent middle knowledge. But when a God endowed with middle knowledge allows some terrible evil to enter our lives, we can be comforted by the knowledge that he has a morally sufficient reason for doing so, and so we can trust him.

My friend Chris Shannon is one such person. Chris was devastated when last year his little daughter lost part of her hand as a result of an accident at school. He told me, "The only thing that I think kept me from completely losing my mind is the fact that I had studied the problem of evil and suffering in the world, and as a Christian, how God relates to this problem, and so I was prepared intellectually to deal with it after the initial emotional barrage." Revisiting the literature on this problem, Chris found the

Molinist view on this problem to be biblical, plausible and very comforting. On [this] view, God is endowed with middle knowledge, which is knowledge of what every person would freely do in any circumstances that person is placed in. So God chose to create a world in which all of the myriad of free choices of people result in God's plan for humanity taking place. This means that people have the freedom to do evil or good and God is not the author of evil. Human freedom is so important to God that He created people with it even though it inevitably leads to bad things happening to us. But, God endowed with middle knowledge can bring good out of the bad things.... I am thankful to God for providing intellectual resources through philosophers and theologians ... to aid those like me who are dealing with such difficult circumstances and using them to draw us closer to Him.[8]

I can understand why people might find the cognitively limited Superman preferable to the all-determining God of Reformed theology, with respect to whom it becomes meaningless to speak of a difference between his direct and permissive will. But the God of Molinism is engaged in the same struggle against sin and suffering that we are. He has to play with the hand he has been dealt. He, too, is grieved at the evil that infects the world. The difference is that he will not permit any suffering to enter your life for which he does not have a morally sufficient reason.

CONCLUSION

George Bailey discovered that when viewed from God's perspective, given divine middle knowledge, it's a pretty wonderful life after all, despite its shortcomings and disappointments. Of course, not everyone can say that— for all too many, life is, as Thomas Hobbes observed, poor, nasty, brutish, and short. But even in such cases, one can take consolation that such suffering occurs only as permitted by God for morally sufficient reasons and is but a prelude to an eternal life of unalloyed joy.

---

[8]Chris Shannon to William Lane Craig, January 29, 2015.

3

An Open Theist View

WILLIAM HASKER

Why do we feel compelled to write about evil? Not, I hope, because evil is inherently attractive and fascinating to us. There are at least three better reasons to write about it. One reason is that many people, perhaps all of us at one time or another, are oppressed by the power of evil in our lives and the lives of people close to us, and we are seeking some sort of meaning or comfort. If we are Christians, we feel compelled to ask about the place—the alarmingly large and prominent place—evil seems to have in a world created and governed by a good and loving God. And finally there is the fact that there are a good many people—philosophers, but also ordinary people little influenced by philosophy—who find in the existence and prevalence of evil a strong reason to disbelieve in God and his good purposes for us.

It is the last of these reasons, in the form of arguments from evil for the nonexistence of God, that prompts much of the writing in books such as this one. But the other two reasons, though they remain distinct from this one, are not unrelated to it. Sometimes it might be possible to block arguments from evil without providing any general account of the place occupied by evil in God's world. But it seems clear that the most satisfying response to such arguments ought to include some sort of overall view of the situation; "defenses" that lack this feature tend to be unsatisfying. And it is also clear that the pastoral task of providing comfort to those who are suffering is distinct from the philosophical and theological task of providing a theoretical account of evil. Nevertheless, the two are not unrelated; one's overall understanding of the reasons for evil and of its place in the world can either help or impede the task of coming to terms with evil in one's own life.[1] The situation is complicated, however, by the fact that individual responses to such considerations vary widely; views about divine providence and about evil in general that one person finds comforting and supportive might be experienced by others as repugnant and as exacerbating the problem.[2] Here as elsewhere, we need to recognize that incontrovertible proof resulting in consensus is likely to elude us, even as we continue to pursue the truth to the best of our ability.

Arguments from evil begin by identifying some particular evil, or class of evils, that are of concern, and then they proceed by way of various premises to the conclusion that a good God would not have permitted such evils to occur; it follows that, since there are such evils, there is no God. There are two main ways in which to respond to such an argument. The most obvious sort of response is to provide an account of the situation that shows (or at least makes it plausible) that God has a morally sufficient reason for permitting the evil in question, thus depriving the argument of its force. Such a response is traditionally termed a *theodicy*, from the Greek words meaning "a justification of God." Another sort of response, however, does not claim to identify God's morally sufficient reason for allowing the evil; rather, it blocks the argument from evil in some other way, often by objecting to one or more of the premises used in showing that God would not permit the evils in question to occur. Such a response is termed a *defense*, in contrast to a theodicy.[3] A defense has the advantage of being less demanding than a

---

[1]The contrast between the two tasks is evident in two books by C. S. Lewis. *The Problem of Pain* (New York: Macmillan, 1947) is an apologetic work comparable to Lewis's other books, such as *Miracles* and *Mere Christianity*. *A Grief Observed* (New York: Seabury, 1969), in contrast, was written in the throes of Lewis's intense grief over the death of his wife, Joy, from cancer. The content of the two books is ultimately consistent, but the tone is understandably very different.

[2]This point is illustrated by Richard Rice's remarkable book *Suffering and the Search for Meaning: Contemporary Responses to the Problem of Pain* (Downers Grove, IL: IVP Academic, 2014). Rice surveys in an evenhanded way seven different philosophical and theological responses to the problem of suffering, showing in each case how the approach provides comfort for some sufferers but also leaves puzzles and unanswered questions.

[3]It should be said here that some authors use the term *defense* differently from how it is defined here. In some cases a philosopher will propose a scenario that, if true, would show that God has a justifying reason for permitting some evil or other. It is acknowledged, however, that the scenario might not be true; it is not known to be true, but neither is it known to be false. For some philosophers, such a scenario counts as a "defense"; I would rather describe it as a tentative proposal for a theodicy.

theodicy; it does not require one to say anything about God's actual or possible reasons for permitting some evil to occur. But also a defense, if relied on to carry the full burden of responding to an argument from evil, tends to be less satisfying than a theodicy, other things being equal. It seems that many of us do have a strong desire to understand, at least in some limited way, the reasons why our world contains so much evil, but a defense as such does nothing to satisfy that demand.[4] The approach I will take here will be that of theodicy.

This essay seeks to address the problem of evil from the standpoint of *open theism.* The term *open theism* came into use subsequent to the publication in 1994 of *The Openness of God: A Biblical Challenge to the Traditional Understanding of God*, by Clark Pinnock, Richard Rice, John Sanders, William Hasker, and David Basinger.[5] It should be noted, however, that the view had already been advocated in its essentials by a number of other philosophers and theologians, for example by Richard Swinburne in his groundbreaking work *The Coherence of Theism.*[6] A central concern of open theists is to maintain a robust realism concerning the character and activities of God attested in the Bible and to present such a view in a framework that is clear, readily intelligible, and philosophically and theologically defensible. We do not advocate a wooden literalism; clearly much that is said about God in Scripture is figurative and requires a nonliteral interpretation. However, we seek to avoid the situation found in some other approaches, in which an acceptance of the biblical witness is substantially undermined by an extremely abstract characterization of God that can only be reconciled with that witness by heroic intellectual gymnastics. In order to make my point clear I offer a single example: The traditional view that God is "pure actuality," lacking any element of potentiality, is very difficult to reconcile with the biblically based assertion that God has done many things that he need not have done and is capable of doing a great many other things that

---

[4]Alvin Plantinga's "free will defense" (see *The Nature of Necessity* [Oxford: Oxford University Press, 1974]) is an interesting case in point here. Plantinga makes it very clear that he is offering a defense and *not* a theodicy, yet a great many critics have insisted on treating it as if it were a theodicy.

[5]Clark Pinnock, Richard Rice, John Sanders, William Hasker, and David Basinger, *The Openness of God: A Biblical Challenge to the Traditional Understanding of God* (Downers Grove, IL: InterVarsity Press, 1994).

[6]Richard Swinburne, *The Coherence of Theism* (Oxford: Oxford University Press, 1977; rev. ed., 1993).

in fact he never does. This is merely one of several assertions often made in traditional theology that is rejected by open theists.

What is it, stated in positive terms, that open theists say about God? We hold, following Anselm, that God is absolutely perfect in power, wisdom, and love; in general, God is "whatever it is better to be than not to be." Our differences with more traditional views concern not the truth that God is perfect but rather the question of what that perfection consists in. God, we say, is eternal, not in the sense of being timeless but in the sense of ever-lastingness: he always has existed and always will exist. God is unchangeable in his nature, but he undergoes changes of state, including God's affective states; he genuinely rejoices when we flourish and sorrows when we suffer, especially when we suffer due to our self-imposed alienation from him. In the words of Clark Pinnock, God is not the Unmoved Mover but rather the "Most Moved Mover."[7] The *relationality* of God is extremely important; God is "really related" to us his creatures, and we are really related to him.

Much of this, to be sure, is held in common with other Christian theists who find such a dynamic, relational conception of God congenial. The most distinctive tenet of open theism, and the one that has generated much of the controversy about the view, is open theism's conception of dynamic omniscience (the term is due to John Sanders), in particular of God's knowledge of the future. We hold that much (not all) of the future is known by God as what *might happen*, and as what *will probably happen*, but not as what *will definitely* take place. And this has important implications for divine providence and for the problem of evil: it means that God is a *risk taker*. When God decides to bring about a particular situation, one that involves his creatures in making free choices, it is impossible even for God to know with certainty how those creatures will respond; there is a genuine possibility that they will not respond in the way he intended and desired for them to do. (Of course, there is much in the Bible that indicates that this not only could but also often does happen.)

My project in this essay, then, is to present a theodicy that is consistent with open theism. I will not be focusing on disagreements with other pro-posals for addressing the problem of evil, such as are presented by the other

---

[7]Clark H. Pinnock, *Most Moved Mover: A Theology of God's Openness* (Grand Rapids: Baker, 2001).

contributors in this volume; those issues will mainly be left for the second essay. However, a bit more needs to be said here about the kind of theodicy that will be presented. A theodicy replies to an argument from evil by giving a justifying reason for the existence of the evil in question—a reason such that, if it obtains, the permission of the evil by God is morally justifiable and does not constitute a reason to disbelieve in God's existence or his goodness. It is unnecessary, and often unwise, for the theodicist to claim that the reason given is the actual reason God has permitted the evil; this might or might not be the case. Now, the justifying reason for God's permission of an evil consists essentially of some good that is made possible, or some evil that is averted, by God's permission of the evil in question. But these goods, or evils averted, might be of two kinds. Suppose the evil permitted by God is a major hurricane striking the Atlantic coastline of Florida, with both damage to property and loss of life. A theodicist might respond by pointing out that the occasional occurrence of such hurricanes is an inevitable consequence of the overall climate system of planet Earth, a climate system that much of the time and over much of the planet's surface produces conditions that are conducive to the flourishing of all kinds of living creatures, including human beings. Call a theodicy that relies on considerations of this sort a *general-policy theodicy*; it justifies God's permission of certain evils as being the consequence of a general policy that a wise and benevolent God might well adopt.

Or the theodicist might take a different tack. In justifying God's permission of the hurricane she might appeal not to general policies such as the maintenance of the planetary weather system but to specific benefits that result, or harms that are averted, by the particular hurricane in question. Call a theodicy of this sort a *specific-benefit theodicy*. The relationship between these two sorts of theodicy requires careful consideration.[8] In one sense, to be sure, there is no inconsistency between the two: it could very well be the case both that the occurrence of the hurricane is the consequence of a wise and benevolent policy with respect to the planetary climate system, and also that there are specific benefits obtained, or harms prevented, by God's permission of the hurricane that could not have been obtained had

<hr/>

[8]The ideas developed here were suggested by some remarks by James Keller. See his *Problems of Evil and the Power of God* (Aldershot, UK: Ashgate, 2007), chap. 5.

the hurricane been prevented. However, the following question needs to be considered: *In justifying God's permission of a particular evil, is it sufficient that the evil is the result of a general policy that a wise and good God might well adopt? Or is it necessary, on the contrary, that God's permission of this particular evil should have consequences that are better than any that could have been obtained had God prevented the evil?* The answer to this question has momentous consequences for the enterprise of theodicy. If the answer to the first question is affirmative, it follows that, strictly speaking, theodicy has *no need whatever* to appeal to beneficial consequences from God's permission of a specific instance of evil. If the evil in question is the result of a general policy that is itself wise and good, that is a sufficient answer to the problem the theodicy sets out to address. To be sure, if there are specific beneficial consequences, they might furnish an example of God's ability to *bring good out of evil*, and this theme is an important element in the Christian understanding of the relationship between God and evil. But theodicy need not rely on such benefits in order to accomplish its task.

Suppose, on the other hand, that a successful theodicy requires that there be a specific benefit from the particular evil under consideration. In this case, the invocation of general divine policies *will never be sufficient* to provide justification for God's permission of a particular evil. This need not mean that the discussion of such policies is entirely pointless; the specific-benefit theodicist might welcome an argument showing that the general policies followed by God in the world's governance are on the whole wise and beneficial. But any argument of this sort necessarily falls short of rebutting the charge that a particular evil morally should not have been allowed by a good God.

It should be evident that an open theist theodicy, which understands God as a risk taker, must be a general-policy theodicy. In a great many instances God cannot know, with certainty, what the consequences of a particular course of action will be, so it is out of the question to make the justification of God's permission of some evil dependent on something that logically cannot be known. It is almost equally evident that a risk-free theodicy must be a specific-benefit theodicy: God, knowing in advance precisely what the result will be of his permission of some evil, can hardly be supposed to ignore that knowledge and base his permission of the evil solely on considerations of general policy. It is my view that a specific-benefit approach creates serious difficulties for views that embrace it, but I will not pursue this topic here.

What sorts of policies, then, should we suppose that God follows in his governance of the world? In answering this question, it is helpful to keep in mind the distinction between *moral evil* and *natural evil*. Moral evil is evil that consists in, or results from, morally wrong choices on the part of morally responsible agents. Natural evil, in contrast, consists of harms of various sorts—suffering, disease, death—that result from the action of natural causes, with no significant role being played by the morally wrong actions of free creatures. The distinction between the two will not always be clear-cut; consider a situation in which the harmful effects of a hurricane are amplified as a result of the culpable failure to make reasonable preparations in advance. Still, the distinction is important, and it will be useful to structure our discussion in terms of it.

NATURAL EVIL AND THE NATURAL ORDER THEODICY

We begin by presenting a theodicy for natural evil. The theodicy begins by setting out some very general, structural features of a world.[9] These features are abstracted from the world in which we live, but they are general enough to apply across a wide variety of possible universes. I claim that we can see that it is *good* that a world with these features should exist. I will then go on to point out that the various forms of natural evil arise as a consequence of these structural features. If it is good that a world should exist with these structural features, it is also justifiable that the natural evils should be allowed to exist; they are, so to speak, the price of admission for the existence of such a world.

First, *it is good that there should be a world.* By *world* here I mean the sum total of concrete things that exist, other than God if there is a God. And to say that it is good that there should be a world is to say that it would *not* be better if, instead of any world's existing, there should be absolutely nothing at all—again, apart from God if there is a God. To say that it is good that there should be a world is an extremely minimal affirmation of the value of existence. The denial of this affirmation, while conceivable in

---

[9]Much of the material in the remainder of the essay is taken from *The Triumph of God over Evil* (Downers Grove, IL: IVP Academic, 2008), chaps. 5 and 6.

the abstract, would be an expression of utter nihilism; for most of us, I hope, such a denial is not merely implausible but virtually inconceivable and is not in any sense a live option. That it is good that there should be a world is of course compatible with the view that it would be better if a world vastly different from this one should exist, so this is only a small first step toward our goal of theodicy.

Here is my second claim: *It is good that there should be a complex, multi-leveled natural world.* This proposition is itself quite complex, but the various ingredients do not readily lend themselves to separate consideration. To say that a world is *complex* is to say that it contains many different entities and kinds of entities, interacting with one another and doing many different sorts of things. To say that it is *multileveled* is to say that the entities exhibit different degrees of complexity, both in their internal structure and, more importantly, in their causal powers; those that are more complex in their structure and powers are thereby "higher" than those that are less complex. To say that the world is *natural* is to say that the entities act, and interact, in accordance with their inherent causal powers, as opposed to being manipulated by some other, presumably "higher," being. (Think of the difference between a puppet show and a group of human beings and animals interacting naturally. The charm of the puppet show, of course, consists in the fact that the puppets, if skillfully handled, are able to simulate many aspects of such natural interaction.)

Of the features mentioned, the idea that a world should be *multileveled* especially invites further exploration. A world that did not exhibit this feature would consist of entities all on the same level in terms of complexity of structure and causal powers. At one extreme, this might be a world simply of "atoms," the simplest, most elementary objects there can be.[10] (This is not the same, by the way, as a world *composed* of atoms and nothing else; such a world might well contain structures of extraordinary complexity. Nothing is said here against that possibility.) I do not suppose there will be much objection to the judgment that a world consisting only of separate atoms would be uninteresting, even boring, if there were anyone around to be

---

[10]The atoms of modern science, of course, are not elementary objects but have a complex internal structure. The word *atoms* is used here simply to represent the simplest elementary components of physical reality, whatever those components might in fact be.

interested or bored. The other extreme would be a world such as George Berkeley's, consisting of rational spirits and nothing else. Notably, however, Berkeley's world contains the *systematic illusion* of a myriad of less complex entities, providing for those rational spirits an arena in which to act and interact with one another. In a positive way, the notion that a world should be multileveled captures something of the sense of the "great chain of being" that was thought to connect God with all of creation; it was important for the completeness of the whole that all the levels of metaphysical excellence—all the "links in the chain"—should be occupied.[11]

Consideration of the atoms-only world suggests a third desideratum: *It is good that a world contain living beings that are sentient and rational.* In thinking about the atoms-only world, we were forced to imagine at least one rational being (perhaps the creator) in order to make sense of the notion that the world could be assigned any valuation. But if the world is good, then it is desirable that it be found to be so by its inhabitants, and surely their appreciation of it will require extensive sensory capacities as well as reason, which is needed to enable the evaluation. Conceivably this desideratum taken by itself could be supplied by a single sort of beings that are both sentient and rational. But a multileveled world will contain beings with graduated arrays of sensory and rational capacities, allowing for a rich variety of ways in which the world can be apprehended and appreciated.

Beyond this, I maintain that *it is good that the creatures in the world should enjoy a considerable degree of autonomy.* Autonomy suffers from a poor reputation in some religious circles, and not without reason. To be autonomous is to be self-ruled, and often this has been taken to imply freedom from all rule by another, even by the Creator. This is not the kind of autonomy I advocate here. Each and every creature is totally dependent on the Creator for its very existence, not only for its original coming-into-being but for sustaining its existence from moment to moment. And the right of the Creator to rule over his creation is not in question. Surely, however, it is conceivable that a being that depends on a superior power, and lies properly within that power's scope of control, should nevertheless in many situations

---

[11]This principle in various forms is assumed by many philosophers, from Plato and Plotinus to Spinoza and Leibniz.

be allowed the freedom to operate according to its inherent capabilities, without direct control or interference by that power. And to the extent that this is done, the intrinsic worth of the being is more clearly exhibited than it would be were this degree of independence not allowed. This is most evident in the case of persons endowed with free will, but there is a good measure of plausibility in applying it to nonpersonal agents as well; much of the fascination of computers and robots, for example, stems from the impression they can give of acting spontaneously, without direction, and producing novel and surprising results. This autonomy acquires an added dimension if, as seems most likely to be the case in our world, there is an element of "chanciness," of indeterminacy, in the fundamental processes of the natural world. It is important, however, to stress that the autonomy praised here is a relative, not an absolute autonomy; the self-activity of the creature is not valued so highly that any special action by the Creator, above and beyond sustaining the creatures in existence with their inherent causal powers, is ruled out as unacceptable.

Finally, I claim that *it is good that there should be an evolving world, a world in which the universe as a whole as well as its component systems develop from within, utilizing their inherent powers and potentialities.* This judgment is obviously dependent on contemporary science; until recently the judgment could not easily have been made, because we knew too little about the developmental history of the world to envisage an evolving world as a realistic possibility. But now we do have that history available—enough of it, at least, to perceive its inherent wonder. The majesty of the Grand Canyon, for instance, is greatly enhanced by the recognition of the hundreds of millions of years of geological history recorded in its successive strata. In this golden age of cosmology, who can help but marvel at the story of the unfolding, since the Big Bang, of the astronomical structures of which our universe is composed? And ever since Darwin there has been the story, still far from complete but continually enriched with new discoveries, of the development of life on this our earth. That this is so cannot be seriously contested. But is it *good* that it should be so? Is a world that has unfolded in this way *better* than if, as our fathers believed until very recently, the major features of the universe, and each separate kind of living creature, had been handcrafted, as it were, by the Creator? Not all will agree on this, to be sure—but I believe that it *is* good, and in support of this I cite earlier thinkers who reached a similar conclusion. Consider, then, these words of Henry Ward Beecher:

> If single acts would evince design, how much more a vast universe, that by inherent laws gradually builded itself and then created its own plants and animals, a universe so adjusted that it left by the way the poorest things, and steadily wrought toward more complex, ingenious, and beautiful results! Who designed this mighty machine, created matter, gave it its laws, and impressed upon it that tendency which has brought forth almost infinite results on the globe, and wrought them into a perfect system? Design by wholesale is grander than design by retail.[12]

Beecher, of course, wrote when Darwinism was in the ascendancy and might be suspected of tailoring his theology to the mood of the times. But similar themes appear in much earlier Christian writers; Gregory of Nyssa, in the fourth century, wrote, "The sources, causes, and potencies of all things were collectively set forth in an instant. . . . Then there followed a certain necessary series, according to a certain order, as the nature of the Maker required, appearing not by chance but because the necessary arrangements of nature required succession and the things that would come to be."[13] It would be difficult to find a clearer expression of the excellence of a world produced by evolutionary development, yet this was written by one wholly innocent of evolutionary science.

Finally, I cite the words with which Darwin concluded *The Origin of Species*: "There is grandeur in this view of life, with its several powers, having been originally breathed into a few forms or into one; and that, whilst this planet has gone cycling on according to the fixed law of gravity, from so simple a beginning endless forms most beautiful and most wonderful have been, and are being evolved."[14]

---

[12]Henry Ward Beecher, *Evolution and Religion* (New York: Fords, Howard and Hulbert, 1885), 114. I am indebted to Michael Murray for this quotation.

[13]Gregory of Nyssa, *Apologetic Treatise on the Hexaemeron*, in Patrologia Graeca 44, ed. J. P. Migne (Buffalo, NY: Christian Literature Company, 1857), column 72. My thanks to Ernan Mcmullin for supplying this reference.

[14]Charles Darwin, *The Origin of Species, A Facsimile of the First Edition* (Cambridge: Harvard University Press, 1954 [originally published 1859]), 490. I believe the point made by Beecher, Gregory, and Darwin can stand on its own merits, but there is an interesting ad hominem aspect to this situation. Theistic believers, whatever their initial predispositions, will find it hard to contest the point, once they are convinced by the evidence that God *has in fact* created the world through an

These features of a natural world are both excellent and beautiful; they are the sorts of features a good and wise Creator might well have chosen to impart to his creation. It is evident, however, that these same features lead, in our world, to the various consequences we denote as "natural evil." Consider, for example, some of the largest and most impressive natural disasters: volcanic eruptions, earthquakes, tsunamis. All of these events can have truly catastrophic consequences; they are often enormously destructive of life forms within the affected areas. These events result from the fact that much of the interior of the earth is in a molten or semimolten state; the earth's crust, to which we cling, is only a thin skin over the inferno beneath. It is also true, however, that the availability of the earth as a site for life depends heavily on these same facts: a planet that was geologically "dead" would have little prospect of harboring life forms like ourselves.[15] To cite one factor among many, a molten interior is a requirement for the earth to have a strong magnetic field, which shields life forms from the otherwise damaging effects of the solar wind and cosmic rays. Furthermore, some of the key transition points in the evolution of living creatures came about as a result of enormous volcanic eruptions, eruptions that were catastrophic in their immediate results but immensely creative in the longer term. These transition points are an integral part of the history that has resulted in the appearance of our own species. As a result of the earth's molten interior we have plate tectonics, resulting in mountain building and earthquakes, volcanism, and tsunamis—and also in the presence on earth of Homo sapiens.

It is evident that similar considerations apply to the phenomena of weather and climate, which are responsible both for an earth hospitable to a vast array of living creatures but also, under some circumstances, for harmful consequences such as hurricanes, tornadoes, and drought. And consider living organisms, the centerpiece of the story. It is immediately evident that organisms are subject to the various kinds of natural disasters enumerated above; indeed, the events would not be termed disasters at all were it not for their devastating effects on life forms. We must also consider the

---

evolutionary process. And nontheists are likely to find it awkward to insist that it would be much better for the world to have been created by a complex series of specific divine actions, rather than allowed to evolve naturally!

[15]For further elaboration, see chap. 3 of Guillermo Gonzalez and Jay W. Richards, *The Privileged Planet: How Our Place in the Cosmos Is Designed for Discovery* (Washington, DC: Regnery, 2004).

need of organisms for sustenance, the energy and nutrients required in order to live, and function, and reproduce. Some highly evolved animals are vegetarian, but many are not; there are significant advantages to be derived from ingesting the highly concentrated nutrients that are available from the bodies of other animals. The general theme of evolution, of course, is that organisms evolve to occupy an available ecological niche, and some of these niches are open to predators and to parasites; disease organisms also have developed so as to exploit opportunities that are available in the ecosystem. All this is to say that the death of living creatures is a pervasive and inescapable feature of any world remotely resembling our own. And once we have complex creatures susceptible to death and harm, pain and suffering are likewise inevitable. It should be noted, by the way, that biological evolution as such does not make the problem of animal suffering any more difficult. On the contrary, it offers some help with the problem, by showing a beneficial result from the pain and suffering that exist in the natural world whether or not we accept that evolution occurred.[16]

These forms of natural evil, then, are an inevitable consequence, in a world such as ours, of the features identified as good and desirable things for a Creator to bring about. The *natural order theodicy* contends that the price was worth paying. This theodicy can be summarized in a series of four propositions:

1. The actual universe is a complex, multileveled natural world, containing creatures that are sentient as well as some that are intelligent. The world has developed to its present state through a complex evolutionary process and enjoys a considerable amount of autonomy in its functioning.

2. The universe so constituted makes possible a large amount of good, both in the order and beauty of the physical universe and in the development and flourishing of a myriad of living creatures. It also unavoidably contains a great deal of suffering and death.

3. There is no good reason for us to suppose that some alternative order of nature, capable of being created by an all-powerful God, would surpass

---

[16]Contrary to some modern authors, the Bible does not in any way view suffering and death in nature as a problem that must be explained away. "The young lions roar for their prey, seeking their food from God" (Ps 104:21 ESV).

the present universe in its potentiality for good or in its balance of good versus evil.

4. In virtue of the first three points, it is good that God has created this universe; there is no basis for holding God morally at fault for doing so, or for supposing that a perfectly good Creator would have acted differently.

MORAL EVIL AND THE FREE WILL THEODICY

The theodicy for moral evil to be presented here is a *free will theodicy*; furthermore, this free will has to be understood in a *libertarian* sense, such that it is genuinely possible, when an agent makes a free choice, for her to decide in any of two or more different ways. Now, libertarian free will is a controversial idea, and ideally the essay would include at this point an extensive discussion and defense of that idea. Space limitations preclude this, so I will say only this much: If libertarian free will is rejected, I see no hope for any remotely plausible solution for the problem of moral evil. Consider this: absent libertarian free will, everything in the universe is exactly as it was planned to be by God, with no constraint on God's choice of a world other than the requirement of logical consistency. Now ask yourself: On this assumption, is it in any way possible, is it even conceivable, that God would be anything but delighted at everything whatsoever that takes place in his creation? To suppose that God would be displeased at something that happens exactly as he planned and intended it would attribute to God a kind of irrationality that is wholly impossible for a supremely rational being such as God is rightly supposed to be. But it is hard to imagine anything that could be said that is more sharply in conflict both with Scripture and with Christian practice than that God is entirely pleased with everything that goes on in his world.

At this point I will set out certain very general, structural features of a "human world." The features are general enough that they might well apply across a broad range of conceivable worlds containing persons, but it would be idle to pretend that we can imagine such alternative worlds except by selecting and/or modifying features familiar to us from human society. So we speak here of a "human world," but we mean to speak about its characteristics in as broad and general a way as possible.

First, *it is good that there should be free, rational, and responsible persons.* This, of course, is a general claim about the goodness of existence that parallels the similar claim concerning the natural world. Here as before, the denial of the claim would seem to amount to a sweeping nihilism, something that might be possible to entertain in the abstract but is exceedingly difficult to embrace sincerely.

Second, *it is good that persons should have occasion and opportunity to develop their inherent potentialities.* Given that persons exist, this seems self-evidently true; it would be absurd to claim that it is a good thing that the persons with their potentials exist but not a good thing that the potentials should be developed and manifested. To be sure, there are in a sense potentialities for evil as well as potentialities for good; the response to this is that the potentialities for evil are merely the perversion of those for good and involve no positive excellence of their own that deserves to be cultivated. These potentialities fall into two broad categories, perhaps inseparable in practice: potentialities for cultural development and potentialities for the development of individual character. Both sorts of potentialities are conditioned by historical circumstances; the former more conspicuously so. Intelligent extraterrestrials observing the earliest members of the species Homo sapiens would have had little evidence on which to predict the proficiency of some later members in non-Euclidean geometry, or the composition of such works as the Ninth Symphony of Beethoven.

A little reflection suffices to show that both sorts of potential require for their development an objective environment, one in which the reactions of surrounding objects to the actions of persons are generally reliable and predictable. What is required, in short, is precisely the sort of environing natural world that was described in the previous section. Obviously there could be no sciences if the world of nature were not reliable in its reactions, and in view of this understandable and predictable. Music is possible because of the reliable acoustic properties both of voices and of the materials of which musical instruments are made; speech itself is possible only because patterns of sound are reliably transmitted through the atmosphere. And as John Hick rightly points out, "The presence of an objective world—within which we have to learn to live on penalty of pain or death—is also basic to the development of our moral nature."[17] This is one of the major themes of Hick's

---

[17]John Hick, "An Irenaean Theodicy," in *Encountering Evil*, ed. Stephen T. Davis, new ed. (Louisville: Westminster John Knox, 2001), 46.

Irenaean or "soul-making" theodicy; in a recent statement Hick elaborates the point as follows:

> We can imagine a paradise in which no one can ever come to any harm. Instead of having its own fixed structure, the world would be plastic to human wishes. Or perhaps the world would have a fixed structure, and hence the possibility of damage and pain, but a structure that is whenever necessary suspended or adjusted by special divine action to avoid human pain. Thus, for example, in such a miraculously pain-free world, one who falls accidentally from a high building would presumably float unharmed to the ground; bullets would become insubstantial when fired at a human body; poison would cease to poison; water to drown, and so on. We can at least begin to imagine such a world. . . . But . . . a world in which there can be no pain or suffering would also be one without moral choices and hence no possibility of moral growth and development. For in a situation in which no one can ever suffer injury or be liable to pain or suffering, no distinction would exist between right and wrong action. No action would be morally wrong, because no actions could ever have harmful consequences; likewise, no action would be morally right in contrast to wrong. Whatever the values of such a world, its structure would not serve the purpose of allowing its inhabitants to develop from self-regarding animality to self-giving love.[18]

It seems to me that Hick is right about this, and that this provides a reason why the existence of a natural environment such as the one in which we exist is a good thing to be celebrated and not an evil to be deplored.

It needs to be said here also that Christian faith contemplates a further goal of personal development, one that lies beyond the cultivation of moral character, though that is an essential component of it. Our true end, it is said, is to "glorify God and enjoy him forever"—to become sons and daughters of God, living in loving fellowship with God and with one another in the enjoyment of God's love. Clearly, this aim is less widely recognized in our society than is the importance of moral character, but for Christian faith it is nonnegotiable.

Third, *it is good that persons be joined together in families, communities, and larger forms of social organization, within which persons are responsible to and*

---

[18]Ibid., 46-47. When Hick first developed the soul-making theodicy, he was a theist of a rather traditional sort. In his later years he was a religious pluralist who took the theodicy to be "mythologically true" though literally false. He still believed, however, that it is the most viable of the various Christian theodicies. See ibid., 65-66.

for each other. These communities are really presupposed in the two desiderata already stated: free and responsible personhood, and the development of the potentialities of persons, are for beings such as ourselves impossible apart from a community of some kind. (Even the hermit has been shaped by the community from which he has departed, and his project is largely determined by his wish to separate himself from it, or at least from some of its aspects.) Higher culture is possible only in a society with a considerable division of labor; the very expression "civilized way of life" refers both to a certain quality of human existence and to the social organization needed to sustain it. But communities and social organization inevitably involve differences of power and status between persons; these might be exaggerated or minimized, depending on the proclivities of a particular group, but they can never be eliminated entirely. The "noble savage," noble precisely because of his independence from organized society, is and must always remain a myth.

Finally, *it is good that the structures and processes of human societies develop from within, utilizing the potentials and the ingenuity of the members of those societies, rather than being imposed from without by a "higher power."* This is of course the counterpart to the "evolutionary clause" in our account of the natural order; it tells us that the structures of human society are precisely *human* structures, the product of human ingenuity and foresight, and that it is good that this should be so. Or would it be better if the structure and organization of society were an "ideal" structure and organization, prescribed from above? It would, however, be the very same, decidedly nonideal individuals who must live in this ideal society and carry out its requirements, and the results could hardly be expected to conform to the perfect ideal. (Consider the uneven success of recent attempts to impose the "democratic ideal" on nations around the globe.) In any case, no single ideal pattern would be feasible; a structure that was the best possible at an early stage of social development would be entirely unsuitable for a more advanced society.

Once again, it is time to draw the threads together and state formally the theodicy developed through our reflections. The free will theodicy comprises five propositions:

1. The world contains persons who are intelligent and free, living in communities within which they are responsible to and for one another.

Human societies have developed by actualizing the inherent potentials of persons and utilizing these potentials for the development of progressively more complex social and cultural systems and progressively increasing control over the material environment.

2. The human world so constituted offers great potential for good in the realization and fulfillment of the potential of human persons and the development of human culture; beyond that, persons have the opportunity to become children of God, enjoying the ultimate fulfillment of which human beings are capable. The human world also offers the possibility, and indeed the reality, of great evil, as persons utilize their freedom to choose evil over good, short-term gratification over the common interest, hatred over love.

3. So far as we can see, no alternative world that does not share these general features could offer a potentiality for good comparable to that afforded by the actual world; only free and responsible persons are eligible to become sons and daughters of God.

4. Frequent and routine intervention by God to prevent the misuse of freedom by his creatures and/or to repair the harm done by this misuse would undermine the structure of human life and community intended in the plan of creation; accordingly, such intervention should not be expected to occur.

5. In virtue of the first four points, it is good that God has created a universe containing human society as described; there is no basis for holding God morally at fault for doing so, or for supposing that a perfectly good Creator would have acted differently.

SHOULDN'T GOD BE DOING BETTER?

Proposals for theodicy such as have been presented unavoidably raise a great many further questions, questions that for reasons of space cannot be addressed here. But there is one general sort of question that we can say something more about. In view of the many and severe evils with which the world is afflicted, shouldn't God be doing better? We are inclined to think there must be *something* more that a powerful and loving God would and should be doing to make the world a better place than it now seems to be. To be sure, one answer is that this "something more" is precisely the Christian plan of redemption—a plan that, we are told, will result in a final triumph of God over evils of every description. This, however, is not our present topic. For our purposes, the question divides into two: Couldn't there be a general plan of creation that provided at least as much good as the present one, with fewer or less severe evils? And couldn't God do more in preventing some of the worst of the particular evils that so trouble us?

As regards the possibility of a better overall plan of creation, it is important to realize that this possibility, if it exists at all, is one of which we have no cognitive grasp whatever. Our failure to grasp such a thing is not a matter of mere ignorance, comparable to our lack of information about some as-yet-undiscovered species of insect. This is a *fundamental* ignorance, and one of the reasons it is so can be found in the phenomenon known as "fine tuning." It is a remarkable fact, widely acknowledged in the scientific community, that many of the fundamental constants of nature are balanced as if on a knife's edge, within an extremely narrow range that is essential for the existence of life as we know it.[19] This fact is not seriously controversial; what is controversial is what should be made of it. Many have argued that such a remarkable combination of improbabilities points to the existence and activity of Something or Someone that has deliberately selected, from all the possible values of these physical constants, the precise combination that makes possible the existence of sentient and rational beings.[20] Needless to say, there is resistance to this suggestion; for our present purposes we have no need to take sides in this controversy. What is important is that, so far as we can tell, there very likely *could not be* a universe with significantly different natural constants than this, in which intelligent observers could live and raise philosophical questions about its existence. True, we cannot absolutely rule out the possibility of a universe radically different from our own, in which the fundamental constituents and forces, and the laws of nature, are completely unlike anything presently within our ken. But anyone who

---

[19]For a readable statement from a scientist who is not a theist, see Martin Rees, *Just Six Numbers: The Deep Forces That Shape the Universe* (New York: Basic Books, 2000).

[20]In addition to Rees's book, important sources for this discussion are John D. Barrow and Frank J. Tipler, *The Anthropic Cosmological Principle* (Oxford: Clarendon, 1986); John Leslie, *Universes* (London: Routledge, 1989); and Neil A. Manson, ed., *God and Design: The Teleological Argument and Modern Science* (London: Routledge, 2003).

would base an argument from evil on a possibility such as this is whistling in a darkness so profound that no light is likely ever to shine into it.

But couldn't God do more in preventing particular instances of evil? Perhaps he could, though we have little insight into what the consequences of more frequent divine intervention might be. The fact is that very often we *just do not know* why certain sorts of evils are permitted by God; that this is so can be a test of faith—sometimes a severe test of faith—for a believer. But for this fact to become the basis for a successful argument from evil, we should need the requirement that *each individual instance of evil* should lead to a greater good or to the prevention of an equal or greater evil. This, however, is a requirement we have already, and rightly, rejected. So yes, we all do wish, sometimes, that God would do more to alleviate the evils that most directly concern us. But this wishing need not, and should not, cause us to doubt God's existence, or his love, or his presence in our lives.

I conclude that the combination of a natural order theodicy for natural evil, and a free will theodicy for moral evil, constitutes an adequate answer to the argument from evil against the existence of God. Whether this is superior, as I believe, to other approaches to this topic is a subject for further discussion.

4

An Essential Kenosis View

THOMAS JAY OORD

*If we are faithless, [God] remains
faithful—for he cannot deny himself.*

2 TIMOTHY 2:13 NRSV

In this essay, I offer a solution to the problem of evil.

Notice I said I will be solving the problem of evil. For many believers, a solution to this age-old challenge is beyond hope. In the face of evil, many Christians settle for a defense to justify their belief in God, rather than a genuine solution to the problem of why a loving and powerful God fails to prevent genuine evil.

The defense many offer involves an explicit or implicit appeal to mystery. "We don't know why God fails to prevent evil," they say, "but we have other reasons to believe a powerful and loving God exists." Instead of offering a robust solution to the primary reason most nonbelievers say they are atheists, defense-playing believers try to show that it is appropriate to believe in God despite this crucial problem remaining unsolved.

I think believers should seek solutions and not merely defenses. In offering my solution, of course, I don't claim to know all things. I see as if looking through a dark glass. No creature is omniscient, because we "know only in part" (1 Cor 13). But I believe appeals to mystery like those we see among mere defenses are not helpful when answering the most important argument against belief in God.

The difficulty of the problem of evil tempts most believers to accept something less than the full solution. In many ways, this is not surprising. A complete solution requires believers to rethink the view of God handed down to them. Yet the work to reconceive, rethink, and reform our views of God in light of Scripture and God's general revelation is the ongoing task of believers.

Reconceiving God is risky business, but it is necessary.

CLARIFYING KEY ISSUES

Let's begin by articulating the problem of evil in a way responsible to the core issues at stake. This articulation might be briefly stated in question form:

Why doesn't our loving and almighty God prevent genuine evil?

The careful reader will notice I use the phrase "prevent genuine evil" in this formulation of the problem. I do this because Christians too often answer the problem of evil by saying God doesn't cause evil; creatures do. But we want to know why a loving and powerful God doesn't *prevent* evil, not just directly cause it. Some say, in fact, that God allows or permits evil, but evil is not God's will. The distinction between God permitting and willing evil, however, is not helpful. I agree with John Calvin that we should make "no distinction between God's will and God's permission. Why shall we say 'permission' unless it is because God so wills?"[1]

In his commentary on Genesis, Calvin puts it bluntly: "What else is the permission of Him who has the power of preventing and in whose hand the whole matter is placed but his will?"[2] If the sovereign God can or does control others entirely and yet permits something to occur, God must *want* that occurrence . . . at least more than the alternatives. A perfectly loving individual would do whatever possible to *prevent*—not just fail to cause or allow—genuine evil.

Let me illustrate: I would not dream of giving my neighbor a Parent of the Year award if he allowed his child to drown in the creek behind our house, saying, "Although I could have prevented the drowning, I didn't *will*

---

[1]John Calvin, *Institutes of the Christian Religion,* John T. McNeill, trans. Ford Lewis Battles (Philadelphia: Westminster, 1960), 3.23.8.

[2]John Calvin, *Commentaries on the First Book of Moses Called Genesis,* vol. 1, Christian Classics Ethereal Library, www.ccel.org/ccel/calvin/calcom01.ix.i.html (accessed Nov. 8, 2016).

it. I just permitted it." A loving parent would do just about everything in his ability to prevent the drowning. My neighbor is morally responsible for failing to prevent this evil.

Similarly, a loving God does not just fail to cause evil. A loving God would prevent genuine evil, if it were possible to do so. The God who could have prevented a genuinely evil event is morally culpable for failing to do so. A steadfastly loving God does not allow preventable genuine evils.

Notice also that I have qualified "evil" with the word *genuine* in much of my discussion thus far. I do so to distinguish between two kinds of events we sometimes call evil. Some events are difficult or painful, but we must endure them to make our lives better. We might call these events necessary evils.

For instance, we all know that the couple who wants children will likely experience suffering in both the birthing and the nurturing of their children. They endure this suffering because they want kids, and they want those kids to have the chance to live life well. The couple endures pain, suffering, and sacrifice—necessary evil—for some greater good.

Genuine evils are different in kind from necessary evils. Genuine evils make the world, all things considered, worse than it might have been. Genuine evils are events that, all things considered, do not make the world a better place than it otherwise could have been.[3] The phrase "than it could have been" suggests that better outcomes were possible should choosers have selected or allowed some other option.[4]

A few believers deny verbally that genuine evils occur. They claim that God allows all things—pleasant and unpleasant, beautiful and ugly, romantic and savage—because they play a part in God's good overall plan. Nothing is genuinely evil, they say, from a God's-eye perspective.

But our day-to-day life betrays the idea that all things are part of God's overall plan. Even though some believers might say genuine evils never occur, they act otherwise. Their moments of regret, guilt, remorse, relief, indignation, and so on suggest they really do think some events are worse

---

[3]I am grateful to David Ray Griffin for introducing me to this general understanding of genuine evil. Among his many books, see especially *God, Power, and Evil: A Process Theodicy* (Louisville: Westminster John Knox, 2004).

[4]I develop the notion of genuine evil in *Defining Love: A Philosophical, Scientific, and Theological Engagement* (Grand Rapids: Brazos, 2010) and *The Uncontrolling Love of God: An Open and Relational Account of Providence* (Downers Grove, IL: IVP Academic, 2015).

than they might have been. In fact, the Christian doctrine of sin implies that we sometimes make choices that are worse than other possible choices. Consequently, we deep down believe genuine evils occur, even if some people deny this with their words.

We who sometimes do evil know something about what goodness entails (Mt 7:11).

FIVE DIMENSIONS FOR SOLVING THE PROBLEM OF EVIL

The solution to the problem of evil I offer has five dimensions. Each dimension is integral to the overall solution, but I will spend the majority of this essay focusing on one. I call it the sovereignty dimension, and it is likely the most controversial. Before I address it, however, let me touch briefly on the other four. No one of these dimensions, by itself, can carry the weight necessary for a comprehensive solution to the problem of evil. But together they solve the problem of evil.

I label the other four dimensions to my problem-of-evil solution as empathetic, didactic, therapeutic, and strategic. The empathetic dimension says that God empathizes with all who suffer. Jürgen Moltmann describes the suffering God well in his monumental work *The Crucified God*.[5] In Jesus Christ's life, suffering, death, and resurrection, we find the revelation that God is affected by what affects us. In the Old Testament, we find numerous references to God interacting with creation and being influenced by creatures.[6] Such suffering love denies the ancient doctrine of impassibility, which says God is unaffected by the joys and sorrows of creation. With most Christian scholars today, I believe God rejoices with those who rejoice and mourns with those who mourn, because creaturely rejoicing and mourning genuinely affect God.

I learned the power of this dimension to my problem-of-evil solution when I was newly married. As a young husband, I discovered that my wife

---

[5]Jürgen Moltmann, *The Crucified God* (London: SCM Press, 1974).
[6]A number of Old Testament scholars describe God as both affecting others and being affected, but Terence Fretheim offers some of the most powerful arguments. See, for instance, *Creation Untamed: The Bible, God, and Natural Disasters* (Grand Rapids: Baker Academic, 2010); Fretheim, *God and World in the Old Testament: A Relational Theology of Creation* (Nashville: Abingdon, 2005); and Fretheim, *The Suffering of God: An Old Testament Perspective* (Philadelphia: Fortress, 1984).

often wanted me to listen and empathize when she experienced conflict, tension, and pain. Empathy was what she needed most. In fact, we all want to know someone feels at least some of what we feel, because we want to know others understand—at least to some degree—what we experience.

In God, analogously, Christians have one who empathizes more fully than any other empathizer possibly could. This is the God whom the apostle Paul calls "the Father of mercies and the God of all consolation." This God "consoles us in all our affliction, so that we may be able to console those who are in any affliction with the consolation with which we ourselves are consoled by God" (2 Cor 1:4 NRSV). God rejoices with those who rejoice and mourns with those who mourn. Although the empathetic dimension plays a significant role in my fivefold solution to the problem of evil, it cannot solve the problem alone.

The didactic dimension in my problem-of-evil solution says that God can use evil to do good in general and build our characters in particular. This does not mean that God causes or allows genuine evil. But God works in and with whatever happens in the world, good or evil, to call creation toward goodness, shalom, or the kingdom of God. God squeezes whatever good can be squeezed from evil events that God did not want in the first place. We can therefore rejoice "in our sufferings, knowing that suffering produces endurance, and endurance produces character, and character produces hope" (Rom 5:3-4 NRSV).

The didactic dimension helps us make sense of testimonies about how suffering and pain have made believers stronger. We can all look back to times when our lives were difficult and see how God used such difficulties to make us better in some way. It is the didactic dimension to the problem of evil that undergirds the popular saying "No pain, no gain."

Unfortunately, some believers use the didactic dimension to claim God causes or allows evil as part of some original blueprint or master plan.[7] If all evil is part of some master plan, those who say rape, genocide, and murder are "God's will" would be correct. The blueprint approach denies that any

---

[7]The most influential form of this argument in contemporary scholarship comes from John Hick, *Evil and the God of Love* (San Francisco: HarperSanFrancisco, 1966). One of the best scholarly criticisms of this view comes from C. Robert Mesle, *John Hick's Theodicy: A Process Humanist Critique* (London: Macmillan, 1991).

evil is genuinely evil.[8] But I find this explanation repugnant. And it makes little sense if God loves perfectly and we have some idea of the meaning of good and evil. Consequently, without the other dimensions to my fivefold solution to the problem of evil to complement it, the didactic dimension can undermine the conviction that God loves perfectly.

The therapeutic dimension to my problem of evil solution says God heals, to whatever extent possible, those who experience injury, destruction, and death. God works with every situation and creature to bring healing to whatever degree achievable, given forces, factors, and other circumstances. Some healing occurs in this life; other healing must wait until heaven.

Healing comes in various forms. Most often, those with expertise in medicine, psychology, or other health care professions are God's primary care providers. But sometimes healing comes miraculously, as God acts specially in unusual ways to do something good.[9] We who endure pain and injury can trust that God works to bring healing.

Solving the problem of evil includes the hope of salve-ation, the salving healing of our sin-sick and evil-torn lives. Whether this healing occurs in our present reality or in the afterlife, we can say with the psalmist, "Praise the LORD, my soul, / and forget not all [God's] benefits— / who forgives all your sins / and heals all your diseases, / who redeems your life from the pit / and crowns you with love and compassion" (Ps 103:2-4).

The fourth dimension I mention briefly points to the role creatures can play in preventing evil. I call it the strategic dimension. God calls us to be colaborers in the strategic work to overcome evil. God's intentions for the good of the world include a necessary role for creatures, especially humans. God asks us to join in the creation project by living lives of love, which means doing good and avoiding evil. This cooperating includes personal, social, environmental, and even cosmological aspects.

I think the Revised Standard Version translation of Romans 8:28 presents well the cooperative nature of the strategic dimension: "We know that *in* everything God works for good *with* those who love him." The two italicized

---

[8]Gregory Boyd is one of the most eloquent critics of the blueprint model of providence. See his essay "God Limits His Control," in *Four Views of Divine Providence*, ed. Stanley N. Gundry and Dennis W. Jowers (Grand Rapids: Zondervan, 2011), 183-208.
[9]I develop a defense of miracles in chapter eight of *The Uncontrolling Love of God*.

words point to the idea that God is active in the midst of all situations. And we show our love for God and others as we cooperate with God's purposes and calling. We are, to use the apostle Paul's metaphor, the body of Christ (1 Cor 12:27), and we are called to be God's fellow laborers in establishing the kingdom (Mt 6:38).

The strategic dimension to my problem-of-evil solution is one of the most important, because solving the problem of evil involves our responses to God's leading. It is hard to overemphasize the role our loving God invites us to take in establishing the reign of love. But even this dimension on its own cannot solve the problem of evil. After all, those who believe a sovereign God can do anything rightly wonder why God doesn't intervene to help victims when creaturely coworkers fail to cooperate with God's good purposes. Saying "we are the solution to the problem of evil" isn't enough.

Having looked at four of the five dimensions to my problem-of-evil solution, I'm ready to address the dimension that will be my primary focus. To explore this sovereignty issue well, let me offer a particular example of genuine evil. I believe that keeping a particular example of genuine evil in mind can encourage us to take with immense seriousness both the grisly reality of some evil events and the great need to reform our view of God.

Let's consider the case of Amy Monroe. Amy was a nine-year-old girl in Wisconsin. She was kidnapped while walking home from school one day. The kidnapper took her into the nearby woods, raped her viciously, and strangled her. A passerby later reported having heard a female voice say, "Please, no! Help me, God!" But the passerby thought the cries were a joke. Searchers found Amy's violated body days later.

It is difficult to hear the story of Amy Monroe and believe that what she endured was not genuine evil. The world surely would have been a better place had she lived and had her rapist and murderer not done his horrific actions. This event was not necessary; this is an example of genuine evil.

The question naturally arises for we who believe in God: Why didn't our loving and mighty Creator prevent Amy's kidnapping, rape, and strangulation?

GOD CAN'T

The sovereignty dimension of my fivefold solution to the problem of evil relies on an idea found at the conclusion of the short biblical passage I offered at the outset of this essay. The verse says this: "Although we are faithless, [God] remains faithful, for he cannot deny himself." The sovereignty dimension to my problem-of-evil solution says that for God to prevent unilaterally the evil done to Amy, God would have to deny himself. But God *cannot* do this. God's nature is self-giving, others-empowering love, and this love is necessarily uncontrolling.

Let me explain.

A good number of Christian philosophers and theologians throughout history have admitted there are some things God cannot do. Most have said, for instance, that God cannot do that which is illogical. God cannot make a round square or a man both a bachelor and married simultaneously. Thomas Aquinas describes this limitation on God this way, "Whatever involves a contradiction is not within the scope of God's omnipotence."[10]

Many theologians have also said God cannot change the past. God cannot change history so that World War I never occurred, for instance. God cannot undue the Nazi Holocaust. In the case of Amy Monroe, God cannot change the fact that she was kidnapped, raped, and murdered. After an event occurs, God cannot alter it, because what's done is done.

Thomas Aquinas is again helpful in explaining this inability on God's part: "Some things . . . at one time were in the nature of possibility . . . but now fall short of the nature of possibility," Aquinas says. Therefore, "God is not able to do them, because they themselves cannot be done."[11] Reverse causation is impossible, even for God.

Other theologians say there are things God cannot do by virtue of what it means to be divine.[12] In fact, biblical writers list some of these limitations on God. For instance, God cannot lie (Heb 6:18), cannot be tempted by evil (Jas 1:12), and cannot become exhausted (Is 40:28). God cannot do these things, because to do them would require God to be something other than deity.

---

[10]Thomas Aquinas, *Summa Theologica*, vol. 1, question 15, article 3 (New York: McGraw Hill, 1963), 163-64.

[11]Thomas Aquinas, *Summa Theologica*, vol. 1, question 25, article 4 (New York: Cosmo, 2007), 139. Jonathan Edwards puts it this way: "In explaining the nature of necessity, that in things which are past, their past existence is now necessary" (Jonathan Edwards, *Freedom of the Will* [New York: Leavitt & Allen, 1857], 10). See also Alvin Plantinga, "On Ockham's Way Out," *Faith and Philosophy* 3, no. 3 (July 1986): 235-69.

[12]Jacob Arminius offers a long list of things God cannot do in "Twenty-Five Public Disputations," in *The Works of James Arminius* (1828; repr., Grand Rapids: Baker, 1991), 1:135.

In addition to the limitations mentioned in the Bible, scholars also typically say that God cannot decide to be 909 instead of triune. God cannot make another God, cannot decide to stop existing, cannot sin, and cannot make a rock so big that even God cannot lift it. These limitations derive from God's own nature, not from some outside force or factor. "When we make such assertions as these," says Jacob Arminius, "we do not inflict an injury on the capability of God." We must take care, says Arminius, "that things unworthy of Him not be attributed to his essence, his understanding, and his will."[13]

All of this means that the idea of limitless divine sovereignty is preposterous.

These are important limitations to God's power, and each is significant for the sovereignty dimension of my problem-of-evil solution. But we can admit that God cannot do the things listed above and yet not have a solution to the problem of evil.

Let's return to Amy Monroe's kidnapping, rape, and murder to see why. Most believers think God's sovereignty is such that God would not need to break the laws of logic to have prevented Amy suffering. Stopping Amy's suffering would not have involved a logical contradiction. Preventing Amy's moment-by-moment horror would also not have required God to change the past. Most believers think God has the kind of power needed to prevent genuine evils as they happen. And, by most counts, preventing this genuine evil would not have required God to have become 909 instead of triune, would not have required God to sin, or would not have required God to do a host of things most scholars say God cannot do by virtue of the divine nature.

One more claim about God's nature is required if we are to understand why God did not prevent the atrocities done to Amy. This claim says God's nature of love makes it impossible for God to withdraw, override, or fail to provide the freedom, agency, or basic existence of others. God's giving of existence to others in love also means God cannot usurp the law-like regularities—what many call "the laws of nature"—we see at work in the world. Self-giving love is an aspect of God's eternal nature, and God cannot deny this nature. Because of love, God must give.

God's loving nature prevents God from unilaterally preventing Amy's kidnapping, rape, and murder.

---

[13]Ibid.

ESSENTIAL KENOSIS

The sovereignty dimension of my problem-of-evil solution is part of a broader model of providence I call "essential kenosis."[14] Many Christians are familiar with the word *kenōsis*, because the verb form of this Greek word appears about half a dozen times in the New Testament. The most discussed appearance of kenosis comes in the apostle Paul's letter to believers in Philippi. Paul writes,

> Let each of you look not to your own interests, but to the interests of others. Let the same mind be in you that was in Christ Jesus,
>
> who, though he was in the form of God,
>> did not regard equality with God
>> as something to be exploited,
> but emptied himself [kenosis],
>> taking the form of a slave,
>> being born in human likeness.
> And being found in human form,
>> he humbled himself
>> and became obedient to the point of death—
>> even death on a cross. (Phil 2:4-7 NRSV)

Theologians interpret this passage in various ways and apply it to various issues. In earlier eras, theologians turned to it when wondering how Jesus is both human and divine.[15] In recent decades, however, theologians appeal to kenosis primarily to describe how Jesus reveals God's nature. Jesus' kenosis tells us who God is and how God acts.[16] Many now read kenosis primarily in light of phrases such as "taking the form of a slave," "humbled himself,"

---

[14]I explain essential kenosis in greater detail in *The Uncontrolling Love of God*. See also my *The Nature of Love: A Theology* (St. Louis: Chalice, 2010), chaps. 4-5; and *Defining Love*, chap. 6.

[15]On the historical debate of kenosis and Jesus' two natures, see David Brown, *Divine Humanity: Kenosis and the Construction of a Christian Theology* (Waco, TX: Baylor University Press, 2011); Thomas R. Thompson, "Nineteenth-Century Kenotic Christology: Waxing, Waning and Weighing of a Quest for a Coherent Orthodoxy," in *Exploring the Kenotic Christology: The Self-Emptying of God*, ed. C. Stephen Evans (Vancouver, BC: Regent College Publishing, 2006).

[16]Among recent helpful texts on kenosis, see Brown, *Divine Humanity*; Peter J. Colyer, *The Self-Emptying God: An Undercurrent in Christian Theology Helping the Relationship with Science* (Cambridge: Cambridge Scholars Publishing, 2013); Evans, ed. *Exploring Kenotic Christology*; John Polkinghorne, ed., *The Work of Love: Creation as Kenosis* (Grand Rapids: Eerdmans, 2001).

and "death on a cross." These passages focus on Jesus' diminished power and service to others.[17]

The kenosis passage suggests that Jesus reveals God's power to be persuasive and vulnerable, not overpowering and aloof. God's power is qualified, others-oriented, and demonstrates servant love. As the "exact representation of [God's] nature" (Heb 1:3 NASB), Jesus' kenosis helps us understand God's nature in light of incarnate love.

The word *kenōsis* sits in the midst of what biblical scholars believe to be a poem or hymn. This genre of literature allows for a wide range of interpretations. Scholars translate *kenōsis* variously as "self-emptying," "self-withdrawing," "self-limiting," or "self-giving."

For a number of reasons, I prefer the translation of *kenōsis* as "self-giving" to the alternatives. I believe it better describes the relational nature of love, both creaturely and divine, described in the larger context of the passage. And it overcomes problems associated with the other translations of the word.[18]

Perhaps the most common contemporary rendering of *kenōsis* pertains to God's alleged voluntary self-limitation. This view says that God, out of love, voluntarily self-limits for the sake of others. John Polkinghorne says, for instance, that "divine power is deliberately self-limited." God essentially retains the capacity to control others but willingly self-restricts. Polkinghorne spells out what voluntary self-limitation means for the problem of evil: "God does not will the act of a murderer or the destructive force of an earthquake, but allows both to happen in a world in which divine power is deliberately self-limited to allow causal space for creatures."[19]

I have already noted problems that emerge when we think God allows evil. The God who voluntarily chooses not to prevent genuine evil is not steadfastly loving. The God who voluntarily self-limits ought to become un-self-limited, for the sake of love, to prevent genuine evil. Kenosis

---

[17]See the work of biblical scholars such as James D. G. Dunn, *Christology in the Making: An Inquiry into the Origins of the Doctrine of the Incarnation*, 2nd ed. (London: SCM Press, 1989), 116; Donald Macleod, *The Person of Christ: Contours of Christian Theology* (Leicester, UK: Inter-Varsity Press, 1998), 215; Ralph P. Martin, *Carmen Christi: Philippians 2:5-11 in Recent Interpretation and in the Setting of Early Christian Worship*, rev. ed. (Grand Rapids: Eerdmans, 1983), 170.

[18]See a full explanation of my reasons in *The Uncontrolling Love of God*, chap. 7.

[19]John Polkinghorne, "Kenotic Creation and Divine Action," in *Work of Love*, 102.

understood as voluntarily divine self-limitation makes God culpable for
failing to prevent genuine evil.

Take Amy Monroe's situation again. The God who voluntarily self-limits
should have become un-self-limited to prevent the perpetrator of Amy's
horrors. Allowing Amy's suffering did not promote Amy's good, the perpetrator's good, or the common good. And yet those who believe God voluntarily
self-limits also believe God could have prevented what happened to Amy.

If Jesus truly reveals God's love, as Philippians and other biblical passages
suggest, we have a strong christological reason to doubt the validity of voluntary divine self-limitation. I cannot imagine that Jesus would stand by
self-limited as Amy was raped and murdered. I cannot imagine Jesus would
say to Amy, "I could stop this. But I think it's best for me to stay out of it."

If I cannot imagine Jesus standing idly by self-restrained while Amy was
raped and strangled, it makes little sense to me to say God would remain
self-limited and not have prevented this evil. After all, I believe Jesus reveals
God's kenotic love.

ESSENTIAL KENOSIS AND EVIL

In light of the problems that kenosis as voluntary self-limitation presents, I
turn to explain how the "essential" in essential kenosis overcomes these
problems. Essential kenosis considers the self-giving love of God revealed
in Jesus Christ to be logically primary and necessary in God's eternal essence. "[God's] steadfast love endures forever," as the psalmist puts it (Ps 136
NRSV), because God's nature of self-giving love is eternal.

Essential kenosis says key limitations to divine power derive from God's
nature of love. The Creator does not voluntarily self-limit, nor does creation
rule its Maker. Instead, God's self-giving, uncontrolling love is a necessary,
eternal, and logically primary aspect of the divine nature. This logical pri-
ority qualifies how God works in and with creation.

The voluntary divine-self-limitation view implies that love is *not* the
logically primary aspect of God's nature. But in essential kenosis, self-giving
love is both necessary and comes first in the divine nature.[20] God relentlessly

---

[20]God is not free to choose *whether* to love, because God's nature is love. However, God freely
chooses *how* to express love in each moment. God is free in this important sense, because in each
moment God freely chooses to love one way instead of another. Love is necessary in God's essence

and essentially expresses love in the quest to promote overall well-being. God could no more stop loving than stop existing. Because God must act like God, God must love: God "cannot deny himself."

The sovereignty dimension of my problem-of-evil solution draws from the essential kenosis claim that God necessarily gives freedom, agency, and law-like regularities to creation. The result is the bold but helpful claim that God *cannot* unilaterally prevent genuine evil. Combining the Philippians passage about kenosis and the Timothy passage about God's inability to deny himself, we can affirm the following:

God cannot deny God's own nature, which necessarily expresses self-giving love.

Essential kenosis says that God always gives freedom, agency, self-organization, and law-like regularity to creation, depending on the complexity of the creatures involved. The gifts God gives are, to use the apostle Paul's language, "irrevocable" (Rom 11:29 NRSV). Out of love, God necessarily gifts others in their moment-by-moment existence, and God cannot rescind these endowments. To do so, says essential kenosis, would require God to deny the divine nature of love.

John Wesley describes this aspect of essential kenosis well. When explaining providence, Wesley says, "Were human liberty taken away, men would be as incapable of virtue as stones. Therefore (with reverence be it spoken) the Almighty himself *cannot* do this thing. He cannot thus contradict himself or undo what he has done."[21]

Because God *must* give freedom and cannot override the gift given, we should not blame God when creatures misuse freedom. Creatures using freedom wrongly are blameworthy. Parenting illustrates this. The rapist's parents are causally responsible for bringing him into the world. Their sexual union made his existence possible. But we would not consider them morally culpable when their son freely chooses rape. We blame the rapist, not his

---

but expressed freely in relations with creatures. I explain this in greater detail in *The Uncontrolling Love of God*.

[21]John Wesley, "On Divine Providence," Sermon 67, in *The Works of John Wesley*, vol. 2 (Nashville: Abingdon, 1985), paragraph 15. Wesley also says that God does not "take away your liberty, your power of choosing good or evil." He argues that "[God] did not *force* you, but being *assisted* by [God's] grace you, like Mary, *chose* the better part." "The General Spread of the Gospel," Sermon 63, in *Works of John Wesley*, 2:281 (italics original).

parents, although the parents were originally responsible for his existence.[22]

In Amy's situation, essential kenosis says God necessarily gave freedom to her rapist and murderer. Giving freedom to all creatures complex enough to use it is part of God's necessary, steadfast, self-giving love. God cannot fail to provide, withdraw, or override the freedom a perpetrator of evil expresses. God must give freedom, even to those who use it wrongly. Consequently, God is not culpable for preventing the horror Amy suffered.

God must give and cannot take away free will.

Saying that God must give freedom and cannot take it away does not solve the problem of evil fully. After all, we could imagine scenarios in which Amy's suffering was prevented and yet God did not withdraw, override, or fail to provide her perpetrator's freedom. Such imagined scenarios might involve changes among small entities or organisms that we doubt possess the capacity to express full-blown freedom. The evil-preventing scenarios we might imagine could involve interruptions of the law-like regularities of nature, or what many call "the laws of nature." Consequently, the sovereignty dimension of my problem-of-evil solution also includes an explanation of why God does not manipulate and control lesser entities or laws of nature.

Essential kenosis says God cannot totally control lesser entities or interrupt law-like regularities and thereby prevent genuine evil. In the case of less complex entities, God necessarily gives the gifts of agency and self-organization. Doing so is part of divine love, because God loves *all* creation. This means God cannot withdraw, override, or fail to provide the agency and self-organizing of any simpler organism or entity. The love of God is also uncontrolling among the less complex creatures and entities of our universe.

Realizing that God cannot unilaterally prevent suffering by manipulating simple entities helps us make sense of what many call "natural evils." This means, for instance, we should not accuse God of causing or allowing birth defects, cancer, infections, disease, hurricanes, earthquakes, tsunamis, or other illnesses and catastrophes. Such calamities do not represent God's will.

Essential kenosis offers a version of what some call the "free process"

---

[22]It is important to distinguish between God's partly causing an occurrence when giving freedom and God's being morally culpable for failing to prevent evil. Because God providentially gives freedom to creatures complex enough to express it, God gives freedom that creatures can use for good or evil (or morally neutral) activities. God acts as a necessary, though partial, cause for all creaturely activity.

response to evil. However, because essential kenosis says God gives agency and self-organization to creation and such giving derives from God's loving essence, it overcomes problems that arise in versions of the free process defense that imply God's gifting is entirely voluntary. According to essential kenosis, the dynamic, sometimes chaotic, and partially random universe, with its various systems and processes, emerges from God's necessarily creative and kenotic love. The free process of life is an essential expression of divine grace.

In the case of Amy's rape and murder, God could not have unilaterally caused her rapist to become intensely sick, blind, or immobile. To do so would have required God to withdraw, override, or fail to provide agency and self-organization to his body's basic organisms, entities, and structures. A loving God who necessarily self-gives cannot do this or interrupt other natural processes. To do so would require God to "deny himself," to use the language of the Timothy passage again.

God's love necessarily gives agency and self-organization.

Essential kenosis says God cannot interrupt the law-like regularities of existence. God cannot do so, because these regularities derive from God's persistent and loving activity in creation. God's love is the source of the existence of all that exists, and God's existence-giving love is irrevocable.

The regularities we witness in our world are not voluntarily inserted by God, nor do they transcend God from the outside. God's loving nature is the ultimate source of creation's law-like regularities, and the God who loves necessarily cannot interrupt the love divinely expressed to all. Rather than being an external watchmaker, God's ongoing, ever-influential love conditions all creation as the One in whom all things live and move and have their being (Acts 17:28).

I agree with Polkinghorne when he says, "The regularities of the mechanical aspects of nature are to be understood theologically as signs of the faithfulness of the Creator."[23] Essential kenosis adds that the Creator's faithfulness derives from that Creator's nature, in which love is logically primary and necessarily expressed to creation. Polkinghorne also says that the regularities described by physics "are pale reflections of [God's] faithfulness

---

[23]In John Polkinghorne, "Providence," *The Polkinghorne Reader: Science, Faith and the Search for Meaning*, ed. Thomas Jay Oord (Philadelphia: Templeton Foundation Press, 2010), 124-25.

towards his creation." Consequently, God "will not interfere in their operation in a fitful or capricious way, for that would be for the Eternally Reliable to turn himself into an occasional conjurer."[24] I agree with Polkinghorne here too. But essential kenosis would say that because God's nature
is kenotic love, God *cannot* interfere with these law-like regularities.

In Amy's case, God could not have unilaterally prevented her rape and
murder by interrupting the law-like regularities we find in nature. Because
God necessarily gives existence to all creation and because God's love for
creation manifests law-like regularities, God alone could not have averted
this tragedy. To prevent Amy's rape and murder by causing a tree to fall on
her perpetrator or suspending the laws of gravity momentarily, God would
need to forgo loving interaction with some portion of creation. Because God
loves *all* creation and God "cannot deny himself," God could not have prevented Amy's suffering by failing to express self-giving, other-empowering,
and existence-providing love.

Divine love necessarily compels God to act in ways that generate law-like
regularity.

ANTICIPATING QUESTIONS

When I explain my fivefold solution to the problem of evil and essential
kenosis, those who hear it often say it makes sense. Essential kenosis carries
through the logic of God's love and creaturely freedom, agency, and law-like
regularity. Of course, those believers reluctant to place any limitations on
God's power—despite what some biblical passages, our experience, and
reason suggest—are usually not open to the essential kenosis view.

Those open to reconceiving God's power in the way I have suggested,
however, often ask two questions in response. I want to answer those questions as I conclude, in part because I imagine my conversation partners in
this book might have them.

The first question has to do with God's being unable to do what creatures
sometimes can do. In terms of Amy's situation, we might ask the question
this way: "We can imagine the passerby who heard Amy's cries walking into
the woods and forcibly stopping the rape and murder. Perhaps the rescuer

---

[24]John Polkinghorne, *Science and Providence: God's Interaction with the World* (Philadelphia: Templeton Foundation Press, 2005), 30.

hit the rapist over the head with a log, knocking him unconscious. Or perhaps the rescuer had a gun and threatened to shoot the rapist if he did not let Amy go. Or perhaps the passerby nonviolently placed her body between the rapist and Amy. If we creatures sometimes thwart evil, why can't a loving God do so?"

To answer this question, we need to look at another way God's power is limited. This answer affirms the traditional Christian view that God is an omnipresent spirit. Those who affirm this view, however, often fail to think through its implications. Being an omnipresent spirit affords God both unique abilities and limitations.

To say God is a loving spirit is to say, in part, that God does not have a localized divine body. God is "incorporeal," to use the traditional language, or as Jesus puts it, "God is spirit" (Jn 4:24).[25] Scripture and tradition have also said that God is omnipresent or universal. Rather than being localized in a particular place in the way creatures are, the Creator is present to all creation.

Believers have tried to describe God as the omnipresent Spirit in various ways. There is a venerable tradition within Christian theology, for instance, that says God is like a mind or soul. This description is helpful in part, because we cannot perceive minds or souls with our five senses. And yet we believe minds or souls have causal influence.

Another analogy says God's incorporeal being is like air or wind. This description is helpful in part, because wind has a physical dimension, although we cannot see it. Wind also exerts causal force. Comparing God to a mind, soul, or wind has biblical justification, and these words emphasize the incorporeal aspect of God's being. But they do not do full justice to God's omnipresence.

All analogies between God's being and creaturely being fail in some way, of course. My main point in exploring God as a loving, omnipresent spirit is to help us see why God cannot prevent evil in the ways creatures sometimes do. As an omnipresent spirit with no localized divine body, God cannot exert divine bodily influence as a localized corpus. This means God

---

[25]Those like me who say God is an omnipresent spirit do not also need to claim God has no physicality whatsoever. We can believe a physical dimension exists in the divine presence, although we cannot perceive it with our five senses. I explore this in a number of publications, but especially in *The Uncontrolling Love of God*, chap. 7; and "The Divine Spirit as Causal and Personal," *Zygon* 48, no. 2 (2013): 466-77.

cannot walk into the woods and use a divine body to stop Amy's perpetrator. God does not have divine hands to grab a log or to put a divine body between Amy and her perpetrator.

God cannot prevent evil in the way creatures sometimes can, because God does not have a localized divine body; God is an omnipresent spirit.[26]

The careful reader will have noticed that I have said "God alone" cannot stop the evil using a divine body. And I have said God cannot prevent evil "unilaterally." I include these important qualifiers, because I believe creatures with hands, feet, and bodies can respond well to God's call and use their creaturely bodies to prevent evil. Of course, creatures can also respond poorly to God's call, disobey, or ignore God's leading. When they do so, God's will is not done on earth as it is heaven.

The second question has less to do with the problem of evil and more to do with how we generally think about God's activities in relation to Christian doctrines. In terms of Amy's situation, we might ask the question this way: "If we say that God's self-giving love cannot stop Amy's murder and rape unilaterally, does this mean we must reject the vision of God's power we find in the Bible, assumed by many throughout history, and apparent in some Christian doctrines?"

Christians intend for Scripture to inform their views of God's action. For this reason, the issue of biblical interpretation plays a key role in how we answer this second question. In response, let me begin by saying that I have no doubt that many have *interpreted* the Bible as describing a God capable of controlling others. This interpretation, however, unfortunately makes God culpable for failing to prevent evil in general and Amy's suffering in particular. And for this reason and others, we ought to look for an alternative interpretative lens.

The challenge as I see it is to interpret the Bible in terms of the overall drift, general tenor, or broad scope of its witness to God and creation. As I and many other Christians read it, the Bible's primary or dominant view is that God's logically preeminent attribute is love. This means we can

---

[26]Depending on one's view of the incarnation, of course, one might think Jesus is an exception to the view that God does not have a localized divine body. That discussion requires a book. But I agree with many theologians who distinguish between God's essential and eternal being and God's temporary incarnation as a localized human, Jesus of Nazareth.

interpret biblical passages pertaining to divine power and might in light of those pertaining to divine love and generosity, especially if, as essential kenosis argues, self-giving love logically comes first in God's nature.

As I read Scripture, the uncontrolling love of God arises as the main and overriding theme. Taking what I find as the central theme of Scripture provides a hermeneutical lens for interpreting the rest. Additionally, I find no biblical passage that explicitly says God entirely controls others. The closest the Bible comes to saying so might be the passages that speak of God hardening Pharaoh's heart, but those need not be interpreted as saying so.[27]

There are definitely passages that say or describe God as almighty. I strongly affirm them. But these biblical passages are plausibly interpreted as describing a God who is *mightier than* all others, is the source of *might for* all others, and exerts *might upon* all others. God can be almighty in these senses without being capable of preventing evil by totally controlling others. We can consistently interpret the overall tenor of the Bible as promoting the uncontrolling love of God. The God who emerges from this interpretation is magnificent, glorious, awesome, and also almighty.

Unfortunately, most of the greatest theologians in the Christian tradition have not taken the uncontrolling love of God as their hermeneutical lens or their primary theme when formulating Christian doctrines. Most have assumed God did, does, and/or someday will entirely control others. Most seem not to have considered the possibility that God's self-giving love comes logically first in God's nature. Few systematic theologians seem to have begun with the conviction that God's nature is love and thought through systematically various Christian doctrines using that orienting conviction.[28]

I believe a robust Christian systematic theology using God's uncontrolling love as its orienting concern can make better sense of Scripture and the doctrines of the Christian faith. To defend and develop this claim well,

---

[27]Other verses in the story say Pharaoh hardened his own heart. More importantly, translators have assumed divine coercion when choosing words like *hardened* to describe God's activity in relation to Pharaoh. But other English words are also viable translations, and these do not have the connotations of coercion that *hardening* can have. See Terence Fretheim, *Exodus*, Interpretation (Louisville: Westminster John Knox, 2010).

[28]I explore some theological failures of those who fail to take the uncontrolling love of God as their orienting concern for their formal theologies in *Nature of Love*.

however, would require at least another book. But let me touch briefly on a few of the issues.

The uncontrolling love of God provides better grounds for the doctrine of original and ongoing creation. After all, biblical writers say God initially created the universe in relation to something, not nothing (Gen 1:1-3).[29] God's uncontrolling love continues to create, and this view of God as Creator is consonant with contemporary scientific theories, such as evolution. The miracles we read of in the Old and New Testaments often describe creaturely cooperation, and sometimes miracles were thwarted because creatures did not cooperate with God's uncontrolling love. God expressed uncontrolling love in the Holy Spirit's inception of Jesus, in which Mary cooperates with God's incarnation plans: "be it unto me," she says (Lk 1:38 KJV). Jesus' life powerfully expresses the uncontrolling love of God, as Jesus cooperates with Abba. In his life and death, Jesus reveals God's kenotic nature, which does not control others (Phil 2:3-7). We can even explain God's resurrecting Jesus from the dead as possible through God's uncontrolling love and the cooperation of Jesus' body and spirit.[30] A participatory view of eschatology emphasizes the view that God's consummating power is love and not total control.[31] From the Holy Spirit inception of Jesus, through his life as God incarnate, in Jesus' death and resurrection, and at the eschaton, we have good reason to believe God's powerful activity always works through uncontrolling kenotic love.

CONCLUSION

I have offered a fivefold solution to the problem of evil. The sovereignty dimension to the solution might be the most controversial aspect. It is based on the essential kenosis notion that God necessarily gives freedom, agency, and regularities to creation, because God's nature is self-giving love. God cannot withdraw, override, or fail to provide freedom, agency, or law-like regularities. God's love comes first, and it necessarily gives.

---

[29]Genesis 1 and other biblical creation narratives always describe God's creating in relation to something (chaos, water, deep, etc.). No biblical passage says God creates from literally nothing. I explain this in my essay "God Always Creates Out of Creation in Love: *Creatio ex Creatione a Natura Amoris*," in *Theologies of Creation: Creatio Ex Nihilo and Its New Rivals* (New York: Routledge, 2014), 109-22.

[30]I argue for a noncoercive resurrection, as Jesus' body and spirit cooperate with God's raising activity, in *Nature of Love*, chap. 5.

[31]I explore this briefly at the conclusion of *Nature of Love*.

God's inability to prevent genuine evil is not based on some exterior force or coeternal demigod. But neither is this inability a voluntary self-limitation. Instead, God's limitations derive from God's nature, in which self-giving love—kenosis—is essential to God and logically primary. God cannot deny this nature of love, because God cannot deny himself.

Essential kenosis offers a plausible answer to why God didn't prevent the atrocity Amy suffered and why God doesn't prevent the countless other genuine evils we witness in our world.

5

A Skeptical Theist View

STEPHEN WYKSTRA

Philosophers, I once heard Nicholas Wolterstorff say, should tell more stories.

What is now called skeptical theism emerged within the discipline of philosophy in the early 1980s. It arose in response to the new "*evidential problem of evil*"—a new style of argument for atheism arising after the collapse of what we now call the "*logical* problem of evil."[1] Philosophers William Rowe and Paul Draper have been key workers on the evidential problem, with Rowe pioneering new paths and Draper taking them in a new direction. The rise of "skeptical theistic" responses is often associated with William Alston, Peter van Inwagen, Alvin Plantinga, and myself. The dialectic between evidential atheology and skeptical theism, because of its increasing connections to other perplexing issues in current mainstream philosophy, has become a rich and lively one.

So-called skeptical theism—like the evidential problem of evil to which it responds—comes in many versions, and it is still evolving. What unites all versions, as I see it, is a twofold claim. First, there is the claim that *if* the God of theism exists, we humans should not expect to see or grasp very much of

---

[1]To a first approximation, "logical versions" of the problem of evil tend to rely on the claim that for an *omnipotent* God, there can never be an outweighing good that makes it "needful" for God to allow evil: omnipotence would always have an evil-free plan B by which such a good could be achieved equally well. In his free will defense, Alvin Plantinga, deepening the insights of Augustine and Aquinas, uses modal logic to argue that this seriously underestimates the "things" falling outside the scope of omnipotence. (Omnipotence not only can't create logically impossible worlds, but also can't create—or weakly actualize—some worlds that are logically *possible*.) Rowe's new "evidential problem of evil" fully absorbed this Plantingian lesson, recognizing that even an omnipotent God can get stuck, as it were, between a rock and a hard place.

God's purposes for divine actions—including the divine actions of allowing or even causing events that bring much of the horrific suffering around us. Second, there is the claim that if the first claim is true, then much of what otherwise looks like strong evidence against theism isn't very strong at all.

To discern the strengths and limits of skeptical theism we will thus need to grapple with some of the new evidential arguments for atheism: these are its *discipline* context. But the roots of philosophical views often go deeper than these arguments, extending to other contexts. When we philosophers write for other philosophers in the professional journals, we often keep the deeper roots hidden—even from ourselves. In this there can be considerable loss. This might mean we philosophers should not just write for the philosophical journals; it might also be why Wolterstorff calls for more stories.

I am here not writing just for fellow philosophers. I will expose some of the deeper roots. And I will tell some stories.

THREE ROOT STORIES

The roots of skeptical theism are both personal and biblical-theological. In his book *Lament for a Son*, Wolterstorff himself tells a powerfully relevant story. I will draw on his story shortly.

■   ■   ■

But first, a story from another person, whom for now I will just call Art. Art writes:

> There are two days in 1963 of which I have detailed memories. The first is November 22. Of events on that day—how we learned that President Kennedy had been shot—almost every American my age has clear memories. The second day, only three weeks later, was December 15. Of some events on that day, perhaps only two people now living have clear memories.
>
> It was Sunday, and it was his forty-second birthday. As usual in our small village of Martin, we walked to church that morning. Nancy says that he held the hand of our little sister, Beth, and skipped to church with her. But after church he didn't feel well. When I came downstairs after changing clothes, Nancy said that Mom had taken him to Dr. Pone's office. I had the usual fourteen-year-old boy's hunger pains, and the three of us started eating

without them. I remember Mom's great roast pork that day, and the mashed potatoes with her wonderful gravy.

As we ate, the siren of the fire department—a hundred feet from our house—began to wail. I thought nothing of it—a fire somewhere, I figured. Only Nancy made the connection: the siren also blows for the resuscitator—and no fire trucks had come roaring out. Yet, between bites, I sang the four title words—"Another Man Done Gone"—from a haunting song on a new Johnny Cash album. Nancy looked at me sharply.

A short time later, Mom came through the door. "Come here, children," she said, gathering us in her arms. And then: "Your father has died."

So tell me, you who know, tell us: why did God take our father then—leaving our thirty-eight-year-old mother to raise her three children alone? In taking him, what was God's purpose exactly? Or did God not "take" him but merely "permit" his death? And this, perhaps, not for any "exact" purpose, but only a general one: because—you might say—it was needful for God's having a world with stable laws, causing rain to fall (when the conditions are right) on the just and the unjust alike, and causing heart attacks to fall (when the conditions are wrong) on young fathers as well as old ones. Is this why?

Tell us, you who know. When you're done, Nancy and I have more things for you to explain.

■　■　■

Alongside the struggle evident in Art's story, we can with profit juxtapose some of Nicholas Wolterstorff's reflection on the problem of evil. A good place to start is his moving memoir *Lament for a Son*, written after his son Eric fell to his death while clambering up a steep slope in Austria.[2]

In one passage, Wolterstorff addresses the view that death is God's "normal instrument" for when "we've lived out the years He has planned for us." "All of you there, I'll send some starlings into the engine of your plane. And as for you there, a stroke while running will do nicely."[3]

Challenging this view, Wolterstorff writes:

---

[2]Nicholas Wolterstorff, *Lament for a Son* (Grand Rapids: Eerdmans, 1987). Related philosophical and theological reflections include Wolterstorff's "Suffering Love," in *Philosophy and the Christian Faith*, ed. Thomas V. Morris (Notre Dame, IN: University of Notre Dame Press, 1988), and his "The Wounds of God: Calvin's Theology of Social Justice," *The Reformed Journal* 37, no. 6 (June 1987): 14-22.

[3]Wolterstorff, *Lament for a Son*, 66.

The Bible speaks instead of God's *overcoming* death. Paul calls it the last great enemy to be overcome. God is appalled by death. My pain over my son's death is shared by his pain over my son's death. And yes, I share in his pain over *his* son's death.

Seeing God as the agent of death is one way of fitting together into a rational pattern God, ourselves, and death. There are other ways. One of these has been explored in a book by Rabbi Kushner: God too is pained by death, more even than you and I are; but there's nothing much he can do about it.

I cannot fit it all together by saying, "He did it," but neither can I do so by saying, "There was nothing he could do about it."[4]

So God didn't *take* Eric's life, actively causing his foot to slip; but neither was God—the God who, as Nick writes later, raised Jesus from death—helpless to prevent it. But if God did not cause it, and was not helpless to prevent it, is there some satisfying explanation of why God, so to speak, just *watched?* Wolterstorff writes:

> Job's friends tried out on him their explanations. . . .
>
> I have read the theodicies to justify the ways of God to man. I find them unconvincing. To the most agonized question I have ever asked, I do not know the answer. I do not know why God watched him fall. I do not know why God would watch me wounded. I cannot even guess.[5]

How then does Nick fit it all together? He writes:

> I cannot fit it together at all. I can only, with Job, endure. I do not know why God did not prevent Eric's death. To live without the answer is precarious. It's hard to keep one's footing.
>
> I can do nothing else than endure in the face of this deepest and most painful of mysteries. I believe in God the Father Almighty, maker of heaven and earth and resurrecter of Jesus Christ. I also believe that my son's life was cut off in its prime. I cannot fit these pieces together. I am at a loss.[6]

■   ■   ■

In 1979 the *American Philosophical Quarterly* published a little paper that would launch the evidential problem of evil—Bill Rowe's "The Problem of

---

[4]Ibid.
[5]Ibid., 67-68.
[6]Ibid., 67.

Evil and Some Varieties of Atheism."[7] As it happens, that same year I also took my first teaching job, at the University of Tulsa, having just gotten my PhD from Pittsburgh in "HPS"—the history and philosophy of science.

The HPS Department at Pitt was an exciting place for a country boy from Hope College to do graduate work. My professors were part of a dynamic movement seeking general models of scientific rationality that fit with, and illuminated, the history of real science. And their own work as historians of science was convincing them that *worldviews*—including the many-stranded Christian worldview—had played key positive roles in the conceptual revolutions of modern science. My professors recognized and appreciated these roles.

But none of them—so far as they let on to me, anyway—had ever felt any personal resonance with Christian faith, and several were militant atheists. My dissertation adviser, Larry Laudan, is without doubt the most charismatic atheist I've ever known. He didn't, as I recall, offer much evidence for his atheism. But as I worked under him, I found myself feeling—and fighting—a strong pull toward atheism.

The struggle had a dimension I could not put words to. At that time I did not know any professionally active Christian philosophers—potential mentors on how to be a Christian and philosopher—with whom to try to give voice to the struggle. I remember sitting in the lobby of a hotel at my first American Philosophical Association meeting, watching Alvin Plantinga and William Alston walk by, desperately wanting to get to know them. But I was awkward—still am. I did not know how—could not find courage enough—to just go up and nervously introduce myself.

At about that time, I happened on Rowe's *American Philosophical Quarterly* paper. In it I found a lucid and forceful expression of *evidence* that might reasonably pull one toward atheism. I became somewhat obsessed with his argument: something, somewhere, seemed amiss in it. Worrying out the

---

[7]William Rowe, "The Problem of Evil and Some Varieties of Atheism," *American Philosophical Quarterly* 16 (1979): 335-41; Stephen Wykstra, "The Humean Obstacle to Evidential Arguments from Suffering: On Avoiding the Evils of 'Appearance,'" *International Journal for the Philosophy of Religion* 16, no. 2 (1984): 73-83; William Rowe, "Reply to Wykstra," *International Journal for the Philosophy of Religion* 16, no. 2 (1984): 73-83. The Rowe-Wykstra-Rowe exchange is reprinted in *The Problem of Evil*, ed. Marilyn McCord Adams and Robert Merrihew Adams (Oxford: Oxford University Press, 1990). Page citations refer to this volume.

argument in my Introduction to Philosophy class at Tulsa, I had a eureka moment—a crucial insight about where the argument went wrong. A year later I was able to test out the insight in conversation with Rowe, as part of his six-week National Endowment for the Humanities summer seminar at Purdue.[8] It held, and I worked out the nitpicky details in several papers. Over the coming decades, Rowe would work at new versions of his argument, and I would work at evolving my basic response to keep up. It continued to hold.

These two men—Laudan and Rowe—were important philosophical conversation partners in my early career. Part of me, I came to feel, was looking to such men for a kind of father. How often, I wonder, do some of us— awkward young philosophers—look for mentors and models from a yearning to earn the privilege of truly knowing and being known by older philosophers we look up to? And how much, I began to wonder, might we be pulled by such "nonrational" factors toward one worldview and away from another? Not long after, in an effort to fight fire with fire—to balance out, I hoped, the nonrational factors—I introduced myself to some leading Christian philosophers.

In this way providence widened my circle of conversation partners and sometimes-mentors. For me and others I've known like me, relationships with such men are important. Yet they remained, almost always, philosophical fathers only. Even as I sit with them and analyze whether human suffering is evidence against theism, rarely do I learn of their real struggles or brokenness, nor they of mine. And understandably so. Few—even among our real fathers, but especially in the world of professional philosophers—feel able to share, to bear, neediness or brokenness in that way. Nor we with them.

So we plow on, cultivating our fields of analysis. Until, perhaps, we fall.

ROWE'S NO-SEE ARGUMENT

As our paradigm example of the new evidential problem of evil, let's grapple with Rowe's classic 1979 paper. Like some of his later papers, it begins by asking us to reflect on a concrete instance of suffering in our world. I will supply an instance of my own, which I saw in a newspaper—perhaps the *Tulsa Tribune*—soon after reading Rowe's 1979 paper. A mother in California,

---

[8]For amusing bits of that story from Rowe's point of view, see the opening of his "Friendly Atheism, Skeptical Theism, and the Problem of Evil," *International Journal for Philosophy of Religion* 59 (2006): 79-82.

holding her baby daughter in her arms, was riding an intercity bus. The bus blew a tire, and a steel cable from the tire ripped its way through the tire well and floor of the bus. Spinning, it wrapped around the baby's foot, jerking the infant through the jagged hole in the floor, to be mangled beneath the wheels.

Such examples are important, infusing lived experience into otherwise pale arguments. In the early 1980s, as a new father, I could gut-wrenchingly imagine how such an event would shatter a parent's heart. "What possible purpose," we can imagine a parent screaming at God, "could require you to allow a horrific event like this?" Or perhaps just to move, as did the young widow of my first story, into a prolonged Stoic numbness: "Thy will be done, O God, not my will; your ways are not our ways; I give you back my husband. But . . . how can I ever trust you with those others I so love—my children?" In either sort of response we might, like Job, remain in conversation with God. But we might also find ourselves in intellectual trial, doubting God's very existence.[9]

Rowe's "evidential problem of evil" helps us see how this can happen. His argument has two strands. The first is empirical, reaching as it were from below; the second, more conceptual, reaches down from above.

The first strand begins from experience. In this world we find many occurrences of horrific suffering for which we—like the mother on the bus— *see no* good that makes it needful for the theistic God to allow the event. That this is so is hard to contest. It's clear, after all, that we see no outweighing good requiring us to let that infant girl die beneath the bus wheels: had you or I been on the bus and somehow foreseen that event about to happen, *we* would without hesitation have intervened, pulling the mother and child out of that particular seat. Is it not equally clear that we see no outweighing good making it needful for *God* (whose omniscience and omnipotence would make it so much easier) to refrain from intervening? We thus get Rowe's first premise—the *See-No* premise, or, for short:

C-No: For many events of horrific suffering in our world, we *see no* "Outweighing Good" (making it needful for an all-powerful and all-knowing God to allow the event to happen).[10]

---

[9]By "God" I—like Rowe—will mean the God of traditional theism, an all-powerful, all-knowing, all-good-and-all-loving Person who created, sustains, and providentially governs our world. The evidential arguments from evil aim solely to support the claim that this *theistic* God does not exist.
[10]My free paraphrase.

But what, inferentially, does this premise give us? In particular, from *seeing no* such outweighing good, can one inferentially get to there *being no* such outweighing good? In other words, from *See-No* can we get to Be-No, or for short (with a nod to Eminem and B Real):[11]

> *B-No*: For many events of horrific suffering in our world, there *be no* "Outweighing Good."

Now C-No of course does not *prove* the truth of B-No. But might it not be *serious evidence* for its truth? Rowe thinks so and in an important series of papers has sought to articulate why. His seminal 1979 paper relies on how we rightly *reason from appearances*. Such reasoning rests on a general principle of rationality that Richard Swinburne calls "the principle of credulity."[12] If, due to the input from some cognitive situation, it *appears* (or *seems*) that things are a certain way, this is serious prima facie evidence that things are that way.[13] Looking at the sky, my wife rightly says, "It appears that we're going to get some heavy rain." This being so, she has serious evidence it is going to rain—she goes back and gets her umbrella. We distinguish two steps in such cases. First, there is a process whereby input from a perceptual or cognitive situation entitles one to an epistemic "appears" claim.[14] Second, there is the step of taking this appears-claim as *serious* prima facie evidence that probably things *are* as they appear to be.[15]

---

[11] As in Eminem's "Love the Way You Lie" ("wasn't ready to be no millionaire") or (with B Real) his "9-1-1."

[12] Richard Swinburne, *The Existence of God* (Oxford: Oxford University Press, 1979), 254-71. On corrections to Swinburne's account, see Wykstra, "Humean Obstacle," section 2.3.

[13] The principle uses *appears* in what Roderick Chisholm calls its "epistemic" sense, as distinct from its phenomenological and comparative senses. For more detail see Wykstra, "Humean Obstacle," 152-55.

[14] In Wykstra, "Humean Obstacle," sections 2.1 and 3.2, I give various examples to show that appears-claims can represent nonbasic beliefs grounded in inferential processes every bit as much as basic beliefs grounded in, for example, perceptual processes. Early Reformed epistemology, while broadening our notion of properly basic beliefs, has for the most part remained stuck in an internalist and strong-foundationalist conception of properly inferential beliefs. For my own effort to get unstuck see "Externalism, Proper Inferentiality, and Sensible Evidentialism," *Topoi* 14 (1995): 107-21.

[15] In other papers—Wykstra and Timothy Perrine and Stephen Wykstra ("Skeptical Theism, Abductive Theology, and Theory Versioning," in *Skeptical Theism: New Essays*, ed. Trent G. Dougherty and Justin P. McBrayer [Oxford: Oxford University Press, 2014])—I have unpacked this notion of "serious evidence" (or "strong evidence") via the notion of "levering evidence." E is levering evidence for P just in case; were one starting out being "agnostic" or fifty-fifty about P, coming to learn E would be weighty-enough evidence to make it reasonable to believe or accept P. Data that is serious or strong evidence in this sense is of course still open to being defeated on gaining yet more data.

Rowe's first strand is thus a two-step inference. He begins from a See-No premise:

C-No: We see no outweighing good making it needful for the theistic God to allow this instance of horrific suffering.

He then urges that this, on reflection, entitles us to an intermediate step that:

Seems-No: There *doesn't seem* (or appear) to be any such outweighing good.

And it is by this route that Rowe (by tacit use of a principle of credulity) thus gets to:

B-No: Probably, there *be no* outweighing good making it needful for the theistic God to allow this instance of horrific suffering.

■ ■ ■

Suppose we accept this inference to B-No. What does this give us? It gives us, Rowe argues, reason to believe that probably God does not exist. Here enters the second strand of Rowe's case, which begins—from above—with reflection on the theistic concept of God as a *wholly good* being. For a wholly *good* being, Rowe argues, would find any instance of horrific suffering, considered *in and of itself*, as an evil—that is, as something that is considered in and of itself undesirable, or of negative value—a *dis*value. A wholly good being, in other words, can neither find positive value in horrific suffering for its own sake nor be merely neutral or indifferent toward it: taking it in and of itself, she must be *against* it. And that means that she—not just God, but *any* wholly good being—will *allow* such horrific suffering only when this *is needful for*—serves an essential role in—promoting or bringing about an outweighing good of some kind. Rowe does not spend much time on this premise, perhaps because it is fully accepted by many thoughtful theists, both past and present. About that Rowe is surely right.[16] Eleonore Stump, endorsing St. Thomas's views in this area, puts it this way:

---

[16]While my own approach, like Stump's, accepts this premise, other theistic philosophers have rejected it. Some—Marilyn Adams and James Sterba, for example—see it as fundamentally wrongheaded, as harboring a consequentialist ethics that in their view is fundamentally at odds with a Christian view of God. Others—Peter van Inwagen, for one—think it is just oversimplified, failing to reckon with possibilities of intrinsic vagueness, assuming instead that there is some sharp "cutoff point," known to God, about exactly which—and how many—instances of horrific suffering God needs to allow to promote some outweighing good.

Many of the constraints on theodicy that are insisted on by contemporary philosophers also operate in Aquinas's theodicy. On Aquinas's views, if a good God allows suffering, it has to be for the sake of a benefit that outweighs the suffering, and that benefit has to be one that, in the circumstances, cannot be gotten just as well without the suffering: the benefit has to *defeat* the suffering. If *per improbabile* something other than suffering—conversations with God, for example—could have brought Samson to the final redemption he has in his story, then, on Aquinas's views, in the story God would not have been justified in allowing Samson's suffering.[17]

◼   ◼   ◼

From the two strands, then, we get the final stage of Rowe's No-God Argument:

No-God 1: If the theistic God exists, then this God—being all-good—allows one of his creatures to undergo horrific suffering only if doing so is needful for the sake of some outweighing good or goods.

No-God 2: For some instances of horrific suffering, there *are* no such outweighing goods.

No-God 3: So the theistic God does not exist.

This final stage is a *deductively valid* argument: *if* both premises are true, then the conclusion—that God does not exist—must be true. The only question is whether we have—through the two strands of reasoning by which Rowe supports each premise, or in some other way—adequate reason to think both premises are true. To the extent that we do, we have good reason to think that God—the all-powerful, all-knowing, and wholly good God of traditional theism—does not exist.

BRIDGE

How might we compare Rowe and Wolterstorff? Both wrestle with the same ancient "Why?" question, as it arises in the face of concrete, life-shattering events. Both hold that there must—if the theistic God exists—be an answer: a wholly good God would allow such events only if doing so is

---

[17]Eleonore Stump, *Wandering in Darkness: Narrative and the Problem of Suffering* (Oxford: Clarendon, 2010), 378.

needful for some outweighing good. Both are unable to find an answer, to see any such good, to—in Wolterstorff's words—"fit it all together." Again, Wolterstorff writes: "To the most agonized question I have ever asked, I do not know the answer. I do not know why God watched him fall. I do not know why God would watch me wounded. I cannot even guess."

In this, however, Wolterstorff remains in fraught dialogue with God, even in God's hiddenness. The challenge, for him, is one of *enduring*—enduring "in the face of this deepest and most painful of mysteries."[18] He resists the inference to there being no point and (hence) no God. To be sure, he feels the pull of that conclusion. But he finds, we will see, resources sufficient to resist it. Those resources will hinge on his sources of conviction that God *is* real—and that if this is so, there must *be* some way it all fits together, even when he cannot see it.

And Rowe's position—espousing what he calls "friendly atheism"—allows for this. While arguing that apparently pointless suffering is strong evidence for atheism, Rowe also avers that it is, like all probabilistic evidence, *defeasible*: it might in some cases be neutralized, even outweighed, by opposing evidence. And such evidence might be indirect: if someone has strong enough grounds for believing God exists, this might—by what Rowe calls the G. E. Moore shift—be indirect evidence that apparently pointless suffering does have a point, despite the No-See data to the contrary. Rowe's contention is that this data is weighty evidence, so weighty that it will take *a lot*, on the other "theistic" pan of the balance, to neutralize or outweigh it.

But *is* Rowe right about this? And is hoping to "outweigh" it really the only—or best—evidential response? Here enters skeptical theism.

THE TWOFOLD CORE OF SKEPTICAL THEISM

So-called skeptical theism, I said earlier, claims two things. The first claim is that *if* God does exist, we humans should not expect to see or grasp very much of this God's purposes. The second is that once we take measure of this, we can see that many things that might seem to be strong evidence against God aren't strong evidence at all.

---

[18]Wolterstorff, *Lament for a Son*, 67-68.

Taking cues from Wolterstorff, we can find both claims expressed in the book of Job. It was Job's friends, Wolterstorff says, who "tried out on him their explanations."[19] Job—like Wolterstorff—finds their answers unconvincing. While refusing to renounce God—to "curse God and die"—Job is eager to bring before God himself the complaint that he's being treated in a shoddy way. But when Job finally gets that chance, God's reply is stern:

> Who is this that darkens counsel
> By words without knowledge?
> Now gird up your loins like a man,
> and I will ask you, and you instruct Me!
> Where were you when I laid the foundation of the earth?
> Tell Me, if you have understanding. (Job 38:2-3 NASB)

God goes on at some length in this vein—rubbing Job's nose, as it were, in the fact that creating and sustaining the universe is no mean feat. And God then puts a question back to Job: "Will the faultfinder contend with the Almighty? Let him who reproves God answer it." And Job's reply: "Behold, I am insignificant; what can I reply to You? I lay my hand on my mouth" (Job 40:2, 4 NASB).[20]

This isn't likely to impress many philosophers. Laying one's hand on one's mouth—in order, I suppose, having shut it to keep it shut—is not our usual métier. And the speech that the author gives to God is, on first reading, not likely to impress many of us. For one thing, we know that our spinning earth doesn't really have foundations, so God seems to need some remedial tutoring on basic astronomy. More deeply, we might see in it a mere appeal to power and hear in it too many fallacies for which we've got Latin names at the ready.

But the author of this ancient book, if behind us in his physics, has much to teach us. Read prayerfully and with the help of good scholarship, the book gives us a narrative in which God neither silences Job nor gives him some single answer, but rather meets him through a complex process that honors

---

[19]Ibid., 67.

[20]And the ancient author, I think, clearly has Job *getting* that this bears on those complaints he was so eager to voice before God. In thinking God had no good reason for allowing the horrific events that have befallen him, Job realizes he has been rash (Job 42:3): "I have spoken of great things which I have not understood, things too wonderful for me to know."

his questions and seeks to restore Job's trust. I will return to some of this complexity. But one "moment" in it, I suggest, is a skeptical-theistic moment. In it, God brings Job and us to a crucial question: *If* our evolving physical universe *is* the creation of one God, an "I am" whom this tradition calls only Yahweh, will there not be a certain, let us say, *disproportionality* between Yahweh's mind and the mind of any of us? The first claim of skeptical theism is exactly this disproportionality thesis—for short, DISPRO:

> DISPRO: If such a being as God does exist, what our minds see and grasp and purpose in evaluating events in our universe will be *vastly less* than what this being's mind sees and grasps and purposes.

Now here I'd like to register a mild complaint against whomever, with the disproportionality thesis in mind, coined the term *skeptical theism* for our (and Job's) position. In philosophy, to be a "skeptic" is to adopt a stance that certain things we ordinarily tend to think we know (or, perhaps, believe strongly and with confidence) are things we *don't* really know (or should *not* have much confidence about). A skeptic about the external world thus thinks that, contrary to ordinary opinion, we don't really know that the ordinary physical world of dogs and cats and tables and chairs really exists. (For all we know, the skeptic will say, it might all be part of "the matrix.") But in affirming DISPRO, is the skeptical theist (or Job) affirming something contrary to our ordinary suppositions?

I don't think so. It's not, after all, that there's some widespread ordinary supposition that we humans can see and grasp *pretty much everything* that God (if God exists) can; it's not that only a few philosophers—those *skeptical theists*—suggest that this is a bit overweening. To the contrary, anyone who reflects a moment on the matter will recognize that if there is a mind that created and sustains this universe, this mind has a vastly greater scope than a human mind. So far as DISPRO goes, a more apt term for our position might be *sensibly humble* theism, and a more apt term for the denial of DISPRO might be *insanely hubristic* theism.[21] It would, alas, take a Prince to change our name to "the Approach Formerly Known as Skeptical Theism." I will settle for adding the occasional prefix: *so-called* skeptical theism.

---

[21]Since it is a conditional claim, it puts the question to theists and nontheists alike.

The second claim of so-called skeptical theism is that if the first claim is true, then many evidential arguments that might seem to weigh heavily against theism do not come to much. Could this be so for the evidential arguments of Rowe, in response to whom my own skeptical theism arose? Of these Alvin Plantinga remarks: "These new arguments of Rowe and Draper are subtle and sophisticated; many deep and interesting topics come up in considering them."[22]

Can some of these arguments really run afoul of something so jejune as the above conditional theistic humility? It's not that they do so in any way that is (for me, anyway) *obvious*. But that's usually the case with "subtle and sophisticated" arguments by smart people: when such arguments have a fundamental problem—some premise or inferential step that is irremediably flawed—the exact location and nature of that problem is often far from obvious.

It is for this reason that I've set out Rowe's 1979 reasoning in some detail. For where, in it, is the fundamental problem? The problem is not obvious. Indeed, we theists shouldn't think it obvious that it must *have* some fundamental problem. Even if theism is true, it's entirely possible, even likely, that we'll encounter *some* data that, for a period of time at least, is serious prima facie evidence against it. This regularly happens for scientific theories we've come to regard as true. During such periods, our best course is simply to acknowledge the problem and ask whether the negative evidence is outweighed by our overall positive evidence/grounds for the theory.

But Rowe's 1979 argument, as I came to see it, *does* have a fundamental problem. And that problem does arise from its conflict with that first "sensibly humble" claim of skeptical theism. The exact location of the problem, however, is subtle and surprising, and is tightly bound up with one of those topics in philosophy that is—as Plantinga put it—"deep and interesting."

ON AVOIDING THE EVILS OF APPEARANCE

The relevant topic in this case was the epistemology of the "appears" idiom. A key premise of Rowe's argument uses the term *appears*, and that same

---

[22]Plantinga continues, we should note: "Upon close examination, however, they fail, and fail resoundingly." Plantinga, *Warranted Christian Belief* (Oxford: Oxford University Press, 2000), 391. Plantinga's entire chapter here is the best treatment I know of that combines a skeptical theist sensibility with lucid analysis of the many-sided problem of evil.

term (and its cognate *apparently*) runs throughout his paper. Here the term *appears* is serving, as we say, an "epistemic" function, and for this reason it came also to figure heavily in mid-twentieth-century epistemology. Now, in ordinary language, *appears* and its cognates (*apparently, seems,* etc.) have a variety of functions, and real people are able to correctly apply these with little effort. But here, as so often, our ordinary idioms can suffer a certain disorientation when applied to nonordinary topics, and it takes considerable reflection to straighten out the confusions.

■ ■ ■

Consider again, then, Rowe's inferential movement. Put concisely, the inference moves from

No-God 2.1 We *see no* point for horrific event E.

to the further claim that

No-God 2.2 So, there *doesn't appear to be* any point for E.

and from this, to yet further claim that

No-God 2.3 So, probably, there *is no* point for E.

Now here it is tempting to think that if there is any fundamental problem, it will be in the move from 2.2 to 2.3. No-God 2.2 looks—on, as it were, first appearance—like a very innocuous claim; it seems to be little more than a paraphrase of No-God 2.1. But reflection shows that appearances here are deceiving. A first thing to see is that in this context "doesn't appear to be" is using "doesn't" in what we might call its ordinary involuted sense. If someone tells you, in a suitable sharp tone, "I don't believe you're telling the truth!" they are not usually saying "I don't have any belief" about the matter. They are saying "I believe you are not telling the truth." So also here, I've argued, close reflection shows that when Rowe asserts No-God 2.2, he is really saying, "There *appears to not be* any point for E." This is a bolder claim than we might first have thought. And it means that the movement from 2.1 to 2.3 is really from

No-God 2.1 We *see no* point for horrific event E.

to the further claim that

No-God 2.2 So, there appears to be no point for E.

to the yet further claim

No-God 2.3 So, probably, there *is no* point for E.

We can now start to see that the movement from 2.1 to 2.2 is by no means trivial. For some things, it is of course a perfectly legitimate inference. If I casually look around a classroom and see no horse in the room, it is entirely reasonable for me to assert, "It appears that there is no horse in the room." But for other things, it's not legitimate at all. If I look casually around the classroom, for example, and see no flea in the room, am I rationally entitled to say, "It appears there is no flea in the room"?

Or think of it this way: you are in a health clinic getting your daily methadone shot, and the health worker drops the hypodermic needle on the floor. She picks it up off the floor, does a close visual inspection of it for contamination, and says—what is incontestably true—"I see no hepatitis or other viruses on this needle." She pauses and then adds, "So, it *appears that* there are no hepatitis or other viruses on the needle—and so it is *apparently* virus-free!" She then adds, as she puts the needle in the syringe and begins to inject you, "So, probably, it is virus free."

Now, in this series of inferences, where has her biggest mistake occurred? It is (or so I have come to think) in the very first move—from "I *see no* viruses on the needle" to "There *appear to be no* viruses on the needle." That move would be very strong for some things (for from seeing no *dog hair* on the needle, say), less strong for others (seeing no *dirt* on the needle), and absurdly weak for others (seeing no *viruses* on the needle).

᠎   ᠎   ᠎

"Doesn't appear" inferences, we've just seen, differ greatly in inferential strength, ranging from very strong to absurdly weak. Our question must be where Rowe's inference falls on this continuum. Here it would help enormously to have some criterion, some test, that we could use on any such inference to gauge its strength. If we think about the cases considered above, one such test suggests itself. For normal, unaided human vision at close range, some things belong to sorts that are quite seeable; dog hairs or fleas much less seeable; and viruses not seeable at all. (Put a bit more precisely, for a certain sort of exercises of unaided human vision, this is so. From a Boeing 727 at thirty thousand feet, horses on the ground are not seeable at all.) What suggests itself is that the *more* some sort of thing is (for a certain exercise of some cognitive faculty) "seeable," the stronger is the inference from not seeing the thing (given a certain exercise of one's cognitive powers) to a "doesn't appear" claim of the sort involved in Rowe's argument.

Based on this general idea, my earliest published response to Rowe proposed a general criterion for evaluating inferences to appears-claims. I called it CORNEA—a somewhat unprincipled acronym for *the Condition Of ReasoNable Epistemic Access:*

> CORNEA: On the basis of cognized situation s, human H is entitled to claim "it appears that p" only if the following condition is met: *it is reasonable for H to believe that given her cognitive faculties and the use she has made of them, if p were not the case, s would likely be different than it is in some way discernible by her.*[23]

We can see how CORNEA works by applying it, first, to the needle scenario. Here the health worker's "cognitive situation" is *doing a careful visual inspection of the needle and seeing no viruses on it.* She makes the claim "*It appears that (p) no viruses are on the needle.*" CORNEA says she is entitled to this only if the above italicized clause is met in the needle case—only if, that is—

> it is reasonable for her to believe that given her cognitive situation, if there were viruses on the needle, the doctor's perceptual experience (or "cognized situation") would likely be different than it is.

But this is clearly not reasonable for her to believe, given the limits of unaided human visual perception. While entitled to say that she *sees no* germ on the needle, she is not—according to CORNEA—entitled to infer the appears-claim. Her visual evidence of seeing no germs is, after all, just what she should expect—given that germs by their nature are unlikely to fall

---

[23]Wykstra, "Humean Obstacle," 85.

within the limits of human visual perception—if there *were* germs on it. Germs or no germs, we'd expect the needle to look the same way.

CORNEA thus seems to fit and illuminate our intuitions about this and many other cases in which we make appears-claims of an epistemic sort.

■ ■ ■

The issue is, then, what verdict it yields when applied to Rowe's inference from No-God 2.1 to No-God 2.2. Is the italicized condition in CORNEA satisfied for this inference?

Here is where the Disproportionality Thesis comes in. Is it at all reasonable to think that if there were a justifying good for a particular evil, then we would likely discern it? In my 1984 paper, I noted that the outweighing good at issue here is "of a special sort: one purposed by the Creator of all that is, whose vision and wisdom are therefore somewhat greater than ours. How much greater? A modest proposal might be that his wisdom is to ours, roughly as an adult human's is to a one month old infant's."[24]

I then related this to CORNEA: "But if outweighing goods of the sort at issue exist in connection with instances of suffering, that we should discern most of them seems about as likely as that a one-month old should discern most of his parents' purposes for those pains they allow him to suffer—which is to say, it is not likely at all."[25]

But if this is correct, then Rowe's See-No inference is faulty at its very first step. From seeing no point for some horrific event, we should not assert that it doesn't appear to serve any point. One should not speak of the data of "apparently pointless suffering." One who does so—if CORNEA's condition is not satisfied—is akin to the health worker who, on eyeballing the needle closely and seeing no germs on it, asserts that "there don't appear to be any germs on it" and who avers that the needle is "apparently virus-free."[26]

---

[24]Ibid., 155.

[25]Ibid., 88.

[26]Ibid., 89. This crucial point continues to be regularly lost on—or resisted by—otherwise able readers, who treat the CORNEA critique as if it grants (or should grant) the claim that there are evils that are *apparently* pointless, resisting only the conclusion that they are *really* pointless. Failure to distinguish the relevant sense of *appears* might be involved here. Cf. Stephen J. Wykstra and Timothy Perrine, "Foundations of Skeptical Theism: CORNEA, CORE, and Conditional Probabilities," *Faith and Philosophy* 29, no. 4 (2012): 375-99.

NEW DIRECTIONS FOR SO-CALLED SKEPTICAL THEISM

There is no one-size-fits-all approach to every type of evidence that might seem to count strongly against belief in God. In its first phase, we've seen, so-called skeptical theism relies strongly on what I've here called "conditional theistic humility"—an affirmation that *if* the theistic God does exist (that is, if mere theism is true), then it is pretty unsurprising that the divine purposes for God's "actions" will often be beyond our ken. This conditional, modest as it is, removes the sting from *some* evidential arguments that might otherwise seem lethal to theism.

But the "some" is crucial here. In its first phase, so-called skeptical theism takes what we might term a "minimalist" approach to evidence evaluation. It asks what is to be expected from "mere theism"—the theistic hypothesis taken, so to speak, straight up—no mixers, no chasers. In both philosophical and personal contexts, I am convinced, this approach has an important place. But to discern that place we must also discern its limits.

In the philosophical context of meeting Rowe-style arguments, a minimalist approach is especially prudent. It will help little to show that Rowe's data is expectable if we expand mere theism by adding to it *further* auxiliary hypotheses devised solely, as it were, to accommodate his data.[27] For while the expanded hypothesis will now fit his data, it is also now more complicated and top-heavy than before. In our personal journeys, too, there are contexts in which, setting to one side doctrinal accretions, we need to think freshly about mere theism compared with its chief alternatives. While "minimalist," such an approach might honor the momentous character of a first step into mere theism.

But to everything there is a season. Once theism has in our personal belief-space come to fill even a mustard-seed-sized volume, it will want to grow. New questions and new possibilities will beckon for exploration. In philosophical contexts, too, some evidential challenges require an approach that is "expansionist" rather than "minimalist." Rowe-style arguments from

---

[27]For a retrospective on the roots of the minimalist response, see the section "Rowe's First Dagger" in my "Suffering, Evidence, and Analogy: Noseeum Arguments versus Skeptical Gambits," in *Philosophy Through Science Fiction*, ed. Ryan Nichols, Fred Miller, and Nicholas Smith (New York: Routledge, 2009), 179-81.

evil are narrowly "inductive" in character, but there is an evidential case for atheism that can also—and I think better—be given "abductive" formulation, so as to compare theism and its worldview alternatives in terms of explanatory power.[28] Such reasoning about worldview hypotheses will use evidential norms that are relevantly similar to those norms by which, in the doing of science, we use data to evaluate scientific hypotheses. What will such norms look like? Here, even for the doing of science, we have a methodological embarrassment of riches (or perhaps tower of Babel). Among both philosophers of science *and* reflective scientists, there is considerable diversity about how to articulate the norms for rational theory appraisal. If anything is clear, however, it is that scientific insight arises from an approach that is "expansionist" rather than "minimalist."

A broadly Lakatosian approach, I've recently argued, has much to offer us here.[29] On this view, rival theoretical conceptions—a wave conception of light versus a particle conception, for example—function as "hard cores" that are, while not themselves testable (they are too vague for that), put to use as "hard cores" of rival investigative research programs. Each program seeks to "expand" its pet conception into a "best version," by a sustained exploration of various auxiliary claims that can be grafted onto the core conception so as to give that conception more explanatory power and more empirical testability. And in Lakatos's "methodology of scientific research programs," the ongoing evaluation of theories has a strongly "diachronic" component, for each research program will generate a series of "versions" of the core theory, and part of the evaluation involves a norm-governed evaluation of this series—a diachronic or "video" evaluation of how the unfolding of the core conception over time, rather than just a synchronic "snapshot" evaluation of any specific version at one time.

A Lakatosian approach, I think, has much to offer our thinking about the evidential evaluation of rival worldview conceptions. On such an approach,

---

[28]Paul Draper has done much to advance an abductive approach (and to chafe at the idea that skeptical theism is relevant to it). Here see his essays in Dougherty and McBrayer, *Skeptical Theism: New Essays,* and those cited in the bibliography to that volume.

[29]I speak of a "Lakatosian" approach because Imre Lakatos's insights, since his untimely death in 1974, have been steadily enriched by others, melding them with ongoing work in Bayesian probabilism and formal epistemology. Cf. Perrine and Wykstra, "Skeptical Theism, Abductive Atheology, and Theory Versioning," 151.

what I've called "mere theism" would be treated as the hard core of a worldview research program, as would the core conceptions of other world-views. Within each research program, these core conceptions would be fleshed out, by worldview research programs, into successive "theory versions," to be evaluated by norms akin to Lakatosian norms, but with due adjustments reflecting the differences between scientific theories and the leading worldview theories. In seeking to flesh out worldviews into their best versions, such worldview inquiry would not dismiss modes of access other than the scientific, including putative witness to divine revelation and divine illumination within theistic traditions, with their impressive commonalities and their problematic contrasts. It would, over time, evaluate the rival worldviews in terms of their diachronic track record, both in heuristic fruitfulness in theoretical insight into our world, but also—what also falls in the province of worldviews—toward practical wisdom in living out one's life prudently but passionately within it.[30]

THE CONSISTENCY QUESTION

I'm suggesting the above as a new direction—a second phase—of skeptical theism. This suggestion is likely to cause raised eyebrows. To some, I expect the new direction will seem quite unrelated, even alien, to so-called skeptical theism. To others, it might seem to contradict its very essence.

For two reasons, I don't see it this way. First, as noted above, *skeptical theism* is a bit of a misnomer: epistemic humility is not, in the philosophical

---

[30]The relation between scientific and worldview (or metaphysical) research programs needs more attention that I can give it here. But the philosophy of science of Lakatos—like that of Karl Popper, which it seeks to supersede—contains seeds of a fruitful relation between the two sorts of theorizing. Such a relation is nicely telegraphed by the final two paragraphs of the 2010 entry on "panpsychism," by William Seager and Sean Allen-Hermanson, in the *Stanford Encyclopedia of Philosophy*, ed. Edward N. Zalta, Fall 2015 edition, http://plato.stanford.edu/archives/fall2015/entries/. While granting that a worldview like panpsychism cannot be put to a decisive empirical test, they write: "Nonetheless, metaphysical views form an indispensable background to all science. They integrate our world views and allow us to situate our scientific endeavors within a larger vista and can suggest fruitful new lines of empirical enquiry (as the example of Fechner's psychophysics illustrates). In particular, panpsychism accords with an approach that rejects physicalist reductionism at the same time as enjoining the search for neural correlates of consciousness, and it sees, or wants to see, a fundamental unity in the world which emergentism denies. Thus it is not a doctrine at odds with current empirical research. It has always been and remains impossible to resist metaphysical speculation about the fundamental nature of the world. As long as there has been science, science has informed this speculation and in return metaphysics has both helped to tell us what the point of science is and paved the way for new science."

sense, a form of skepticism. Moreover, what so-called skeptical theism asks of us is conditional theistic humility: it asks us, at bottom, to think very seriously about what is to be expected *if theism is true*—about what possibilities are *integral* to theism. The same holds for any worldview core: if the *generic* worldview is true, then it is true in some more specified *versions* (and not in others). Consider, for example, a materialist/naturalist worldview that, put generically, says this: "All that exists, at bottom, is *matter*." If this worldview is true, it might be true on a version that says this matter has existed eternally, *or* on a version that says matter has existed only for a finite period of time. Both possibilities are integral to naturalism, and a naturalistic research program will seek to flesh both out so as to discern which, over time, yields the most empirically and theoretically progressive program. The same holds for other leading worldviews—theistic, panpsychist, and so on. Because the conditional epistemic humility enjoined by so-called skeptical theism reflects an underlying commitment to *integral* theorizing, it is a natural complement to what I am calling "the second phase" of skeptical theism.

What of the second worry—that there is here an actual contradiction? This arises, I think, from arguments that skeptical theism, in its peculiar applications of conditional theistic humility, must logically drive us to more extreme forms of skepticism. The arguments here are too varied and complex to be treated in any detail. But their general thrust, to a crude zero-eth approximation and in "toy" form, might perhaps be put as follows. Suppose, the critics say, skeptical theism is right: all those plentiful and apparently pointless horrific evils are allowed by God because this serves some fabulous outweighing goods that God alone can see and grasp. If we admit that, says the critic, must we not also admit that, for all we know, there might be similar outweighing goods for the sake of which this God has allowed us to be deceived—*Matrix*-style—every time we use our physical senses? And must we not admit that, for all we know, our moral judgments that certain evils are to be prevented by us (by, say, calling 911) are in fact events that God wants to happen for the sake of some hidden outweighing good? And must we not admit that what things we rightly take to be "disclosed" by God through divine revelation are in fact false but taught to us by God for the sake of outweighing goods that God alone can grasp?

If I thought any of these things follow from the core claims of so-called skeptical theism, I would be worried. But I am not: I think that in fact they do not follow at all. Do I mean that I can spot weaknesses in each and every argument given by critics? No. In fact, I can't. But that doesn't worry me much, either. For it just seems to me obvious that conditional theistic humility about *how much* or how *often* we humans should expect to see or grasp the purposes of any God capable of creating and sustaining our universe is entirely *compatible* with holding that we are nevertheless *capable* of seeing and grasping a great many truths about God and God's purposes. It seems obvious enough to convince me that any argument to the contrary has gone wrong somewhere, even if I cannot say exactly where.

If this strikes you as somehow rash, perhaps an analogy will help. We—you and I—are, I imagine, fully convinced that the number of stars in the universe *vastly* exceeds what we are able to see. Nevertheless, we take this as perfectly compatible with our conviction that, when gazing up at a dark sky on a clear night, we are able (at least with a pair of corrective eyeglasses) to see a very goodly number of them. Now suppose we were to learn that there are a number of sophisticated arguments that these two things are incompatible—that if we want to keep one of the two convictions, we must abandon the other. We would surely—and rightly—judge that each argument has gone wrong somewhere, and we would judge this even if we could not, for some or all of them, say exactly where.

The parallel strikes me as complete. "For now," says St. Paul, "we see in a mirror dimly, but then [we shall see] face to face" (1 Cor 13:12 NASB). In its minimalist phase, skeptical theism says only that God's purposes—if the theistic God exists—vastly exceed what we are able to see. In positing conditional theistic humility as something having a claim on any reasonable person and thus as a constraint on evidential arguments against theism, it engages in "negative apologetics." In its *constructive* phase, skeptical theism seeks to explore whatever fraction of God's mind and heart to which we might have progressive access, bringing this into relation with discernible features of our world and our lived experience of it, and any sources of divine disclosure that have rightful claims on our assent. This constructive phase—also a mode of integral theism—uses reflection on our world and ourselves to learn more about God, and reflection on God to get deeper insight into ourselves and our world. In the interim period between St. Paul's "now" and "then," a *constructive* skeptical theism can thus be at once both epistemically humble and passionately investigative—seeking more light, while fully expecting that light to bring surprising revisions, to leave a great many things seen in a mirror dimly, and to leave many more not seen at all.[31]

RESOURCES UNDER TRIAL

And in this interim period, *some* pieces of counterevidence might seriously count against theism, as against *each* of the leading rival worldview theories. That is how incomplete evidence has regularly worked for even our best scientific theories. Why not for worldview theories as well?

Thus it was, perhaps, for Wolterstorff, who, unable to "fit it all together"—unable to "even guess" God's purpose—acknowledges that "to live without the answer is precarious. It is hard to keep one's footing."[32] And a few pages later:

> I am at an impasse, and you, O God, have brought me here. From my earliest days, I believed in you. I shared in the life of your people: in their prayers, in their work, in their songs, in their listening for your speech and their watching for your presence. For me your yoke was easy. On me your presence smiled.
>
> Noon has darkened. As fast as she could say "He's dead," the light dimmed. And where are you are in this darkness? I learned to spy you in the light. Here in this darkness I cannot find you. . . .
>
> Will my eyes adjust to this darkness? Will I find you in the dark—not in the streaks of light which remain, but in the darkness? Has anyone found you there? . . . Or in the dark, is it best to wait in silence?[33]

---

[31]Here I must respectfully disagree with Eleonore Stump, who sees a sharp opposition between skeptical theism and the magnificent project she undertakes in her *Wandering in Darkness*. Stump's brief contrasts of her position with our approach (e.g., 13-14; 408) might suggest to readers that, on our approach to human cognitive limitations, humans are precluded from having *any* access to *any* of God's reasons for allowing suffering. Not so, as this paper endeavors to make clear. Closer to the mark are earlier writings in which Stump affirms that skeptical theism, without precluding our efforts to discern God's purposes, can serve important roles in "taking up the slack" when no account seems adequate. It's also worth noting how Stump herself, in her final pages, hedges her own claims. She thinks that her Thomistic account might well capture—in a "general way"—the *full* range of goods for which horrific suffering is, by God, allowed and guided to afflict any given "fully functional adult human being." But she also explicitly refrains (476) from taking a stand on whether these goods explain the *full* panoply of horrific suffering in our world, including as it does sentient beings who are not fully functional adult humans.

[32]Wolterstorff, *Lament for a Son*, 67.

[33]Ibid., 69.

Wolterstorff does not lose faith; he remains in conversation with God. But one senses his worldview has entered a new period of trial. "Faith," he writes,

> is a footbridge that you don't know will hold you up over the chasm until you're forced to walk out onto it.
>
> I'm standing there now, over the chasm. I inspect the bridge. Am I deluded in believing that in God the questions shouted out by the wounds of the world has its answer? Am I deluded in believing that someday I will know the answer? Am I deluded in believing that once I know the answer, I will see that love has conquered?[34]

If there is genuine intellectual trial here, it is no wonder. Unable to see why his God would allow Eric's fall and all the other wounds of the world, Wolterstorff knows that if there is no God—if it is all a sound and a fury signifying nothing—then loved ones regularly falling to their death, or getting crushed in senseless accidents, is *exactly* what one should expect. And as a good Bayesian will tell you, this must count, to *some* degree, as evidence that counts against theism.

It makes sense, then, when a few pages later Wolterstorff writes: "Why don't you just scrap this God business, says one of my bitter suffering friends. It's a rotten world, you and I have been shafted, and that's that."[35]

But here Wolterstorff is not left speechless, with no reason for the hope that is within him:

> I'm pinned down. When I survey this gigantic intricate world, I cannot believe that it just came about. I do not mean that I have some good arguments for its being made, and I believe in the arguments. I mean that the conviction wells up irresistibly within me when I contemplate the world. The experiment of trying to abolish it does not work. When I look at the heavens, I cannot manage to believe that they do not declare the glory of God. When looking at the earth, I cannot bring off the attempt to believe that it does not display his handiwork.
>
> And when I read the New Testament and look into the material surrounding it, I am convinced that the man Jesus of Nazareth was raised from the dead. In that I see the sign that he was more than a prophet. He was the Son of God.[36]

---

[34]Ibid., 76-77.
[35]Ibid., 76.
[36]Ibid.

Thus it is that despite being quite unable to see how it all fits together, Wolterstorff resists sliding to Rowe's conclusion. I am struck by the role of Jesus here. Every worldview finds something in our experienced world to pick as the "best window" affording what it takes as a glimpse of the heart of reality. A naturalist like Peter Atkins finds the window in his beloved second law of thermodynamics, in which he sees a guarantee that the last word on life will be death—the entropy-death of the entire physical universe. Wolterstorff fixes his eyes elsewhere. He does not know the answer as to why God "just watched Eric fall." But in the life, death, and resurrection of Jesus of Nazareth, he finds ample ground to endure—to believe that "in God the question shouted out by the wounds of the world has its answer," and that for Eric's death, "someday I will see the answer"—and will also, in that day, "see that love has conquered death."[37]

I am struck, too, that in finding that resource in Jesus, Wolterstorff seems to deviate just a little from that Reformed epistemology that treats our access to such things as properly basic belief, rather than evidentially grounded. His conviction about Jesus seem to focus on the witnesses to Jesus' resurrection, and it arises, he says, "when I read the New Testament *and look into the material surrounding it.*" There is, I would like to hope, at least a trace of evidentialism in how Wolterstorff describes the resources sustaining his faith under trial.[38]

BEYOND ANSWERS

We must not, I've argued, expect there to be any one-size-fits-all answer to every parcel of counterevidence that seems to count against theism. Neither should we expect, when in the midst of life-rending events, to find in skeptical theism much balm for grief, or even much help in just enduring. To the contrary, the "theistic" part of skeptical theism, especially if we are in a living theistic tradition, will have given us *expectations* of God as our heavenly Father, and our journey will have brought us, in some measure, to care about things that God cares about. All of this can make our grief and suffering a source not just of grief but of much else—of intellectual questions, of course,

---

[37]Ibid., 77.
[38]Cf. Stephen Wykstra, "'Not Done in a Corner': How to Be a Sensible Evidentialist About Jesus," *Philosophical Books* 43, no. 2 (2002): 81-135.

but also of directing toward God our theistically driven disappointments, protests, even accusations. Theism, if I might so put it, is not for sissies.[39]

Earlier I urged that conditional theistic humility is one important "moment" within the complex narrative of Job's climactic encounter with God. But we—we philosophers, especially—must resist the temptation to reduce this ancient text to a "single-answer" book.[40] Lindsay Wilson's recent book *Job*, weaving many strands of recent Job scholarship into his own treatment, brings into focus how Job's "strong words of protest addressed to God" seem "to sit most awkwardly with his earlier piety." And Wilson then raises an important question: "Can true faith include such statements, accusations, and protests, or has Job overstepped the boundaries of genuine piety?"[41]

As I read Wilson, a fundamental lesson of Job is that such protests are indeed part of genuine faith and piety. When God draws close to Job, his words—"Gird up your loins like a man" (Job 38:3 NASB)—are not meant to make Job cower or silence him. Rather, they exhort Job to stay in bold conversation—even as God pushes back. Recent scholars thus find in this wisdom book a form of "protest wisdom"—in which such protests, as Wilson puts it, "are not seeking to dishonor or denigrate God, but to bring Job's legitimate concerns and questions before his creator. . . . In this sense, Job belongs with the Teacher as boundary rider, not huddling around the central religious community, but listening to the challenges and questions posed by the world."[42]

But if Job is a "boundary rider" for the community, he is also on a journey in his own relationship with God. And at some level he realizes this. Throughout the book, Wilson observes, it is Job alone who prays. Unlike his four friends—Eliphaz, Bildad, Zophar, and, entering late as a young man's voice, Elihu—it is Job alone who, in the dialogues, talks "not only about God but *to* God." And this reflects his realization that it is "the loss of his former

---

[39]No insult intended: some of my best friends are sissies.

[40]I am deeply indebted to my theology colleague John Schneider for giving me a kick in the pants and some useful pointers that led me to incorporate a larger view of Job.

[41]Lindsay Wilson, *Job* (Grand Rapids: Eerdmans, 2015), 249.

[42]Ibid., 297. Wilson's discussion of protest wisdom here draws on William S. Morrow, *Protest Against God: The Eclipse of a Biblical Tradition*, Hebrew Bible Monographs 4 (Sheffield: Sheffield Phoenix, 2006), and on Anson Laytner, *Arguing with God: A Jewish Tradition* (Northvale, NJ: Aronson, 1990).

personal relationship with God that is Job's chief lament."[43] In Job's climactic encounter with God, Wilson notes, God thus "does not respond to each of Job's accusations, apparently understanding that Job's deepest need was not to have an intellectual answer to his many questions."[44] Neither answering Job's questions nor squelching them, God means Job to remain in conversation. And God's long list of questions seems meant not to intimidate but to intimate to him a deeper perspective on the richness of aims that are part of God's relations—gently dialogical *personal* relations, as Eleonore Stump perceptively explains—to other parts of creation.[45]

Now such intimations, as Wilson says and we skeptical theists will second, do not come close to putting Job in an intellectual position to see God's motives in allowing the events that Job and his loved ones horrifically suffered. The prologue, of course, locates these motives in God's transactions with Satan, in which issues about divine honor seem to be at stake. But in the narrative, Job gets no glimpse at all of this—and any glimpse that we might think we get (as readers of a sacred text) serves mostly to bring out how, even with divine revelation, our knowledge of such things falls short of completeness. So, in that divine encounter, I take Wilson to be right in saying that God's intimation of larger purposes is in service not of a theodicy but of enabling Job "to trust God in a new way." Above all, perhaps, Job learns that God had not abandoned him. He was not alone.

■　■　■

And Job's friends, for all their limitations, are also, I think, a positive part of this process. Here I return to the story told by "Art," who, some might have guessed, is "Artsky W. Evets," a somewhat inverted alter ego of Steve Wykstra who occasionally makes philosophical appearances. Each year in deep winter, my sister Nancy and I talk on the phone about that mid-December Sunday in 1963 when John Richard Wykstra's heart stopped beating. Lately we've found ourselves recalling details of how, that afternoon as well in the days and weeks to follow, the people from the

---

[43]Wilson, *Job*, 370. In this last clause Wilson is quoting R. Norman Whybray, *The Good Life in the Old Testament* (London: T&T Clark, 2002), 139.
[44]Wilson, *Job*, 370.
[45]Stump, *Wandering in Darkness*, 188.

Martin Reformed Church came by to be with us. They shook our hands, hugged us, sat with us; they offered their support and their cupcakes and their casserole dishes. A few would stumble out words like "God's ways are mysterious" or "His ways are not our ways." They did not, however, offer long theistic discourses, skeptical or otherwise. And rightly so. For what made a difference, I now realize, was not what they said but that they were there. In the loss of my father, they were tokens, signs—small incarnations, as it were—of God's presence with us. The body of Jesus had been broken for us. The body of Christ was being broken with us. We were not abandoned. We were not alone.

It hasn't always *felt* that way. On the scale of human sufferings, the loss of a still-young father is by no means at the "horrific" end. But my dad was a quiet and complex and still-in-progress man. He left me with much to treasure, but the severing of our relationship, even as I was entering the trials of early adolescence, made for its own complexities and ambiguities. Had he lived longer, some of these might have resolved themselves in ways less fraught for those I most love.[46]

Yet, in the visits of those church folks in Martin, and in the considerable string of father figures and big brothers who, along various stretches of my path since then, have walked with me, I now see, though in a mirror dimly, seeds and signs and semaphores. Seeds of grace-gifted healings come since and yet to come. Signs of someday seeing face-to-face, in Wolterstorff's words, how "in God the question shouted out the wounds of the world has its answer." Semaphores of that new "access to the Father" that in Christ, as St. Paul says to the Ephesians, has come to those who were far away and to those who were near (Eph 2:17). An access, I dare to hope, in which all our human father-failings might yet find healing and forgiveness, and in which our human father-hungers might yet find their final fulfillment. So if asked on this day how I myself most seek to expand and confirm theism, my answer in Christ would be: I expand it thus.

---

[46]Then again, maybe not.

PART TWO

RESPONSES

6

The Classic Response

PHILLIP CARY

The trouble with theodicies is that they can explain too much. They aim to block the inference from the existence of evils to the non-existence of God, by showing that there can be good ("morally sufficient") reasons that justify God in not preventing evils. In that very narrow sense the evils, while genuinely evil, are *justified*, not gratuitous. Most theodicies hesitate to be too specific about what these reasons are. Even so, they might go too far in justifying evils. G. W. Leibniz, who gave us the modern project of theodicy in the first place, is a case in point: having argued that God has the best possible reasons for permitting evils in this best of all possible worlds, he insists that "we must truly be satisfied with everything that has come to us" rather than complaining about God's will.[1] But to chide those who complain is to close off hope for something better, and it is to refuse to pray the demanding biblical prayer of hope, "How long, O Lord?"

So wise theodicies will not be too ambitious. They will be hesitant in offering reasons that justify God, lest they be bereft of reasons for hope. The arguments they give, if they are to be Christian, need to be open to the possibility of a story—the story we actually live in—that moves us from complaint in the middle of the story to rejoicing at the end. For the problem of evil requires more than an argument blocking the inference that God does not exist. It requires a reason to hope that God will make things different from what they now are. This is not just a pastoral or emotional requirement, but a logical implication of any Christian theodicy, for the reasons that

---

[1]G. W. Leibniz, *Discourse on Metaphysics*, §4, in *Discourse on Metaphysics and Other Essays*, trans. Daniel Garber and Roger Ariew (Indianapolis: Hackett, 1991).

justify God in permitting evils are precisely the reasons for hoping that he will bring a greater good out of our present evil. By the same token, these reasons must not offer us the kind of comfort that would make us too comfortable in the present. They must not be such as to make us satisfied with the justified evils of this present time.

"I reckon that the sufferings of this present time are not worthy to be compared to the glory which shall be revealed in us," says Paul (Rom 8:18 KJV). Thus Christian theodicies are situated eschatologically, between the times: between a "now" when evils are in a very narrow sense justified (for God does have his reasons) and a "not yet" in which evils are overcome—because they are in fact hideous and unacceptable, justified now only because they are to be defeated in the future. They will be swallowed up in a victory that reveals their meaning in a way that transforms them, as Easter transforms the meaning of Good Friday. So a theodicy that is too adept at justifying evils cannot be Christian, and a theodicy that is Christian will never finish the job of justifying evils. It must await a solution it cannot give itself, a glory that will be revealed only when the kingdom of God comes on earth as in heaven. Until then every Christian theodicy must be unsatisfactory, reflecting the deeply unsatisfactory nature of evil itself.

■   ■   ■

Thomas Jay Oord's solution to the problem of evil looks to me like one of those theodicies that explains too much. Instead of a reason why God permits evils, he gives us a reason why God can't prevent them. And it is not a hidden reason but one fully accessible to us, based on a firm understanding of God's "nature of love." This is a rationalism more ambitious than Leibniz's.

It also attributes a startling powerlessness to the divine nature of love. In place of the voluntary self-limitation that many kenotic theologies see in God, Oord posits an essential kenosis, a necessary self-giving that forever limits God in very substantial ways, implying among other things his inability to interfere with human freedom and agency or the law-like regularity of creation. Like process theology, this gives us a theodicy that plays by the rules of naturalism—which is reason enough, in my view, to find it questionable. But what is more serious, it attributes to God less power than belongs to anyone who can pick up a stick and swing it at the head of a man about to rape a little girl in the woods. I have never seen what is worth preserving about the freedom and agency of such a man, and neither can I see anything loving or "self-giving" in someone who would refuse to pick up the stick and swing it. Oord himself admits that he can't imagine Jesus, the exemplar of kenosis, failing to intervene. So precisely at this point the concept of kenosis fails to explain why God cannot prevent evils, and Oord must turn instead to the odd notion of an omnipresent spirit that cannot accomplish what anyone with a healthy human body is capable of: putting up resistance to the free agency of a criminal about to do something horrible to a child.

The problem can be generalized. If God can't rescue a little girl, how can he can redeem the world? There is no point praying "How long, O Lord?" to a God who cannot prevent evils. As Oord argues, this is a God we cannot blame or accuse or find culpable. But it is also a God who cannot give us a story in which we can cry out for a final defeat of evils. That, I think, is the price we pay for a theodicy that gets God completely off the hook. He is not responsible for evils, not even for permitting them. But that's because he is metaphysically incapable of putting a stop to them. Better to join Job, I'd say, and hold God responsible: keep him on the hook, and keep complaining like the psalmist until kingdom come.

One small point that reveals much about the radicalism of Oord's proposal is his unusual conception of "genuine evil." By this he means an evil that is not necessary for a greater good, one that by implication is not justified by any good God can bring out of it. It simply makes the world worse. This is what William Lane Craig, using more standard vocabulary, calls "gratuitous evil." I'm with those who think that if such a thing exists, then God doesn't. In the standard vocabulary, the evil that God is justified in permitting is genuine, and the greater good that justifies him in permitting it does not mean it is less than genuinely evil. *Gratuitous* evil is something different, and something worse: it is evil that is not justified, for which there is no reason—which is to say, there is no good that comes of it, no hope for its ultimate defeat or redemption. To affirm the existence of such evil is, to my mind, a counsel of despair.

A more important difference between the classic view and Oord's theodicy has to do with the notion of kenosis itself. As Oord notes, earlier theologians turned to the kenosis passage (Phil 2:7, where Jesus "emptied himself") to think about the incarnation—how Jesus is both God and man. This is quite different from modern "kenotic" theologies, which look at Jesus as a revelation of what God is like rather than as God himself in person. The classic view of evil, of course, is allied with this earlier, robust doctrine of incarnation, in which Jesus' human lowliness does not reveal divine powerlessness but rather is the freely chosen humility of God himself, who descended from heaven not by ceasing to be Almighty God but by taking up our frail, mortal humanity and making it his own. In a formula Augustine loves to use, in many variations: remaining what he was, he took up what he was not.[2]

This has consequences that contrast with both Oord's view and Hasker's open theism. The eternal Son of God, who is true God, remains what he was: almighty, impassible, immortal, while also taking up our vulnerability and suffering and death and making it his own. Hence it is the impassible, immortal God who suffers and dies on the cross. Not all the church fathers were happy to come to this conclusion, but it was the orthodox outcome of several centuries of debate about the doctrines of Trinity and incarnation, all of which took for granted the immutability and impassibility of the divine nature. It is a both/and that I think encapsulates what the gospel of Jesus Christ has to say about the suffering of God.

We are in an era that has much sympathy with Dietrich Bonhoeffer's notion that "only a suffering God can help." The church fathers were of a different mind: they thought only a God free from suffering and death could rescue us from suffering and death. It's as if you were to see people drowning in deep water. It would be a mistake to suppose that only someone who's in the water with them can help. The most reliable rescue comes from someone who is standing on firm ground and can hold out a pole or throw in a lifesaver. Of course, remembering the doctrines of Trinity and incarnation, we do have to make the story a bit more complicated than that. God the Father, standing on the firm ground of his own eternity, throws his beloved Son into the water with us like a lifesaver, and we pull him down into the depths with us, and he drowns. But in the resurrection the Father pulls him out,

---

[2]See for example sermons 184.1, 186.2, and 187.3, in Augustine, *Sermons 148-229Z*, trans. Edmund Hill, OP (Hyde Park, NY: New City Press, 1993).

together with all who cling to him. And the bond of love that connects the Father with the Son and all who cling to him is the Holy Spirit. This is how the triune God does not merely suffer our death but defeats it. Kenosis, in the classic view, means God voluntarily shares our helplessness in the face of death, only in order to overcome it by the power of divine love.

■ ■ ■

William Hasker does the contributors to this book a favor by situating his theodicy in relation to a range of other possible theodicies. His approach is more modest than Oord's and wears its unsatisfactoriness more on its sleeve, which I appreciate. You can see what it does and doesn't aim to accomplish by comparison with other theodicies. Hasker wants to do more than merely block the inference to God's nonexistence, but less than explain why God permits this or that particular evil. He wants to understand something of the place of evil in the world by identifying a "general policy" that justifies God in permitting the *kind* of evils that we see, without identifying "special benefits" that would constitute the greater goods that give God reasons to permit *particular* evils. So he does not tell a particular story but sketches broad structures of the natural and human worlds that make a place for many kinds of evil. A great strength of his approach is that the general structures he identifies are open to particular stories about how God brings a greater good out of particular evils. It is like building a stage for any number of possible dramas.

Where the classic view demurs is at Hasker's contention that the stage is good enough in itself to justify all the evils that take place on it, even apart from the particular drama that God is staging. It is true, as Hasker says, that a good world will inevitably be vulnerable to evil. Augustine thinks this follows from the very ontology of creation, since only God is incorruptibly good (*Confessions* 7.12.18). But since God freely chose to create the world, I would add that he has responsibilities to defend his vulnerable creature from harm and rescue it from evils. That requires a particular story about how the world's Creator is also its Redeemer. Only that particular story can make sense of the particular evils we actually experience. General-policy considerations are insufficient.

The insufficiency is especially clear when we turn to the pastoral dimension of the problem of evil, which, as Hasker points out, is not unrelated to the other tasks of theodicy. Theodicy rightly aims to provide us a kind of comfort, he argues, because understanding the place of evil in the world can help us come to terms with evil in our own lives. But I would emphasize that the logic goes the other way as well: the reasons that comfort us are logically necessary for the success of theodicy, because any reason that justifies God's allowing evil a place in the world must be a reason to hope that we live in a story in which God is doing something that will ultimately defeat evil. General-policy considerations are insufficient because they are about how things do not change, whereas the reasons that justify God in permitting evil must include reasons for expecting that things will be different. And for that we need a story.

So I am not satisfied when Hasker argues that there is "no basis for holding God morally at fault," as he puts it (twice, in the third point of the summaries at the end of his sections on both the natural and the human worlds). In part this is because I am wary of any argument that seems to get God off the hook. God is not culpable, to be sure, but he *is* responsible (by Hasker's reckoning, as opposed to Oord's) for permitting a great many evils. So if we are to trust him, we must be able to hold him responsible for making a future that is different from our present afflictions. That's one of the reasons we pray. And that in turn means we can always undermine the conclusion in the third point by asking, "Couldn't God do better?" The question is intelligible and indeed necessary for all who await a future in which God *does* do better. By a biblical reckoning, the Lord God is the covenant partner of all who believe in him, which means he has promises to keep, and we are longing for the day when we will see for ourselves that he has kept them all. Until then, the particular evils we suffer will from time to time give us reason to worry, to lament, and to complain that God does not appear to be true to his word, and no general-policy considerations are sufficient to keep us from complaining. God can count on hearing our complaints, for he has given us the Psalter to pray.

A deeper reason I am not satisfied with Hasker's theodicy stems from a key feature of open theism: the belief that God takes risks. If he takes risks, then sometimes he loses. On this view, as I suggested in my contribution, he is like a general who is sure to win the war in the end but cannot possibly do so without casualties. And the casualties are what Oord would call "genuine evil" and I would call "gratuitous evil." They are particular evils that serve no particular redeeming purpose; they are lasting and irreversible defeats for God. I think we should hold God responsible for making sure that in the end—seen in the light of the happy ending of the story of the world—there are no evils of that kind.

＊　＊　＊

William Lane Craig's arguments are mainly concerned with blocking the inference to the nonexistence of God, although he does give us some hints about how he sees the overarching story of the world. His Molinist approach includes a robust conception of providence that is closer to the classic Augustinian view than what we find in Hasker and Oord, and for precisely that reason it is worth making the difference clear. However, I think the sharpest disagreement I have with Craig might concern how he sees the story of the world.

In common with the classic view, Molinism holds that God does not take risks. His providence is meticulous: he knows all the evils that will come to pass to the end of time, and they can only come to pass because he permits them. He has good reasons to permit them, because he knows what greater good he will bring out of them. But his reasons are hidden from us, mainly because the whole sweep of history is far too vast for us to be in a position to grasp what God is up to in allowing particular evils. In all this, the Molinist is a good son of Augustine, as Molina himself was.

Molinism departs from Augustine, however, in assuming that only "libertarian" free will (as contemporary philosophers call it) is genuinely free and in building a doctrine of providence around that assumption. Libertarian free will places limits on God's providence that Augustine did not see, for it means (according to contemporary Molinism) that there are *counterfactuals of creaturely freedom*, true propositions about what particular people would have freely chosen to do in particular circumstances that could have taken place but didn't. These propositions are neither necessary truths nor contingent on the creative will of God. They are part of the cards God is dealt, in Craig's metaphor. The cards limit God's options, for they imply that not every possible world is one God could feasibly actualize. But an advantage comes with the limitation, because God knows what all these cards are by virtue of his "middle knowledge," which includes a complete grasp of all the counterfactual propositions of creaturely freedom.

Those of us who are not Molinists find these propositions very strange indeed. A counterfactual of creaturely freedom is a surd, for there is nothing in the world or out of it that causes it to be true—not God's will, nor even the free will of the person who does the choosing. It is just the sheer fact of the matter (to use a famous hypothetical example of Plantinga's) that if a particular politician named Curley were offered a sufficiently hefty bribe, he would take it, whereas he would spurn a lesser amount.[3] Even Curley doesn't choose that this is the truth about Curley's free will. It just is. Those of us who are not Molinists find it hard to believe there are such totally inexplicable truths.

Moreover, according to Molinism, God has to work around this truth if he wants to preserve Curley's free will. He has to play the cards he is dealt, governing the world so as to achieve his own ends by making use of what he knows people will freely do in the circumstances he providentially arranges. So he arranges things so as to put Curley in circumstances in which he will take a bribe—or not—depending on God's good purposes. Thus human free will, about which God knows all the details through his middle knowledge, becomes a kind of instrument, the means God uses to achieve his ends. In this way, despite its reverence for free will, Molinism makes God look like a great manipulator. He leaves our will inviolable, even sacrosanct, but gets us to do what he wants by putting us in circumstances that he knows will result in our freely making choices that fit his plan.

From an Augustinian perspective, the freedom to do evil is not so sacrosanct. Indeed, it is not freedom at all, but a failure to be free. Moral evil is related to the free will as blindness is related to the eye's power of vision. It certainly can happen, but it is an ontological defect, not the exercise of freedom or any other power. It results in bondage to sin (as Paul puts it in Rom 6:6), because it means the will can no longer do what it was created

---

[3]Alvin Plantinga, "The Free Will Defense," in Alvin Plantinga, *The Analytic Theist* (Grand Rapids: Eerdmans, 1998), 38-39.

for, which is to love and enjoy God together with our neighbors. (Craig's notion that we were not created for happiness is bizarre, from the standpoint of the classic view shared by Augustine and Molina, and he must almost immediately take it back by noting that true fulfillment and eternal happiness consist in knowledge of God—which, the Augustinian tradition would add, is a union with God that is inevitably bound together with love as well as joy.)

Since moral evil is a failure of free will, God does us no harm by correcting it—healing our corrupted and impaired wills as a doctor heals a diseased body. This is what Augustinians mean by the word *grace*, which is not only compatible with our free will but also necessary for restoring its freedom to make good choices. Hence, for the Augustinian tradition, the grace of God that turns the sinful will back to the good is opposed only to sin, not to free will. However, this is not the libertarian view of free will that Craig holds but a version of what contemporary philosophers call compatibilism.[4] It means that certain forms of agency that modern thinkers label "free" are in fact forms of corruption and bondage, like the activities of a criminal or the inclination of a sinner to sin. These are not abilities God is obliged to protect, any more than a doctor is obliged to protect our ability to go blind.

So on the Augustinian view God does not manipulate us, using our free will as means to his ends, but rather heals our wills so that we might be happy, which is the good for which he created us. Since he is already the eternal Good, he has no need of any good we could offer him, which means that in giving us grace it can only be our good he is seeking. We were made for his glory, which means we were made for our own happiness.

The happiness he seeks for us is a common good, which Scripture calls the kingdom of God. Hence when God gives grace to one person it might well be for the benefit of others (as Abraham is chosen "for the blessing of all nations" in Gen 12:3). But when God permits *evil*, the greater good he brings out of it must also be good in the end for the one who suffers it. As extravagantly unlikely as it seems, Christian hope must anticipate that in the glory of the kingdom Dostoevsky's tortured children (remember, they were real children, their stories taken from Russian newspapers) will

---

[4]For more details, see Phillip Cary, "Augustinian Compatibilism and the Doctrine of Election," in *Augustine and Philosophy*, ed. Kim Paffenroth et al. (Lanham, MD: Lexington Books, 2010), 79-102.

be able to praise and thank God with glad hearts for the goodness of the life he gave them.

This hope evidently differs from the shape of world history as Craig sees it. Craig suggests that one reason God permits atrocity, disaster, and mass starvation is so that there might be more Christians in the end. If this were about the persecution of the martyrs, whose vindication is glorious, that would be one thing. But Craig's suggestion appears to go further. I hope I misunderstand him, but he appears to think that the sufferings and death of millions are worthwhile because it led to *other* people, later, being saved. If that is the suggestion, then Craig's thinking depends on a kind of instrumental reasoning—more of God the manipulator, using people for his own ends—that would surely justify Ivan Karamazov in turning in his ticket.

* * *

Of all my co-contributors, I find myself most in sympathy with Stephen Wykstra. This has less to do with the essentials of the classic view than with my narrative-inflected way of adding particular details. I fill in the blanks of Augustine's doctrine of grace by following Martin Luther's understanding of the gospel as the story that gives Christ to all who believe it. I agree with Nicholas Wolterstorff, my own teacher, that philosophers should tell more stories. But of all the academic disciplines, I think only theology is in a position to tell the best story of all, for only theology can be captive to the gospel of Jesus Christ. So philosophers' stories are bound to be a bit more skeptical, since their discipline lives by critical thinking rather than by the gospel. But *Christian* philosophers will of course want their stories to be open to that greater and better story. It's the shape of that openness that I want to explore in response to Wykstra.

Skeptical stories have a lot going for them. They show us why a consideration of "general policies" is not sufficient to give us hope. Their focus on particular suffering, in which God's reasons for permitting evils are most hidden from us, is apt to keep us from trying to explain too much. Their skepticism, like the anguish in the biblical genre of complaint, is not inclined to let God off the hook. And the narrative form itself tends to resist too-easy dichotomies such as that between the intellectual problem of evil and the emotional problem of evil. Stories—not least those in the

Bible—show us we need reasons for hope that must engage both our intellect and our emotions.

Skeptical stories have so much going for them that I am strongly inclined to agree with Wykstra that his skeptical theism is better described as "sensibly humble theism." But I am also interested in a different, more theological kind of humility, which Augustine associates with faith in authority. ("Authority" in the Augustinian tradition, I should mention, is an epistemological rather than a political concept. Kings have power, but only teachers have authority—as when we speak of a teacher who "is an authority on her subject.") Humility, in this sense, is the willingness to believe what you're told by someone who knows better than you.

An Augustinian believer aims to move from faith to understanding: you start by believing what Christian authorities teach but end up seeing for yourself. For Augustine this meant seeing God in the kind of intellectual vision that the Catholic tradition later calls "beatific" (i.e., it makes you happy). But in order to arrive at this beatific understanding you must begin with faith, which requires the humility to believe what you are taught by external authorities, especially the prophets and apostles bearing witness to Christ in Scripture. Augustine illustrates the need for this right after telling us of his inward ascent to catch a brief glimpse of the being of God (*Confessions* 7.17.23). He could not maintain this philosophical vision because of his impure heart (for it is the pure of heart who see God, according to Mt 5:8). And he could not attain a pure heart so long as his pride stood in the way of embracing the external authority of Christ incarnate, as he explains in one of the most beautiful lines he ever wrote: "I was not humble enough to hold on to my humble God Jesus."[5]

This theological humility is, to use Wykstra's terms, expansionist rather than minimalist in its claims. Yet it too provides a kind of "hard core" for an ongoing research program. Instead of "God exists," the hard core is the primal Christian confession that "Jesus is Lord." The resulting research program is not a new proposal but the whole Christian tradition itself, which has been learning what it means to confess Jesus as Lord for some two thousand years. The enrichment of the concept of a Lakatosian research

---

[5]This is my attempt at the impossible: an adequate translation of Augustine's wonderful Latin, *non enim tenebam Deum meum Jesum, humilis humilem* (*Confessions* 7.18.24).

program to encompass a whole tradition is central to Alasdair MacIntyre's epistemology.[6] It suggests a way of understanding our own stories, including our intellectual autobiographies, as belonging to a much larger story that grows out of the gospel itself, by the work of the Holy Spirit in the historical life of the church, which includes not just intellectual inquiry but also liturgical practice, ascetic discipline, and works of love.

Yet to return to my Lutheran form of Augustinianism, I would suggest that the understanding at which the tradition is always aiming is less like an inward intellectual vision than like grasping the meaning of a story when we come to the end and see why it is all good. The happy ending reveals that the middle means something more, different, and better than we realized. We can call Good Friday good because of what Easter Sunday reveals about its true meaning. And we will understand why the history of the world is a good story—that it is in fact the fullness of the story that is told in the gospel of Jesus Christ—when we see what is revealed when the kingdom of God comes to us on earth as it is in heaven. This, I think, is why we can be humble enough to embrace the extravagant hope that even Dostoevsky's tortured children will be able, with glad hearts, to praise God for the life he gave them. You don't have to be Lutheran to get the point. It's what Julian of Norwich hears Jesus promise when he tells her, in her vision: "You shall see yourself . . . that I shall keep my word and make all things well."[7]

---

[6]See Alasdair MacIntyre, "Epistemological Crises, Dramatic Narrative and the Philosophy of Science," in *The Tasks of Philosophy* (New York: Cambridge University Press, 2006), 3-23, and compare his account of "The Rationality of Traditions," in chap. 20 of Alasdair MacIntyre, *Whose Justice? Which Rationality?* (Notre Dame, IN: University of Notre Dame Press, 1988).

[7]Julian of Norwich, *A Revelation of Love*, ed. Marion Glasscoe (Exeter, UK: University of Exeter Press, 1976), §31-32 (my translation).

7

The Molinist Response

WILLIAM LANE CRAIG

My interlocutors are primarily concerned with nonlogical versions of the intellectual problem of evil, versions that lie at the heart of the contemporary debate and to which a Molinist perspective on providence is most relevant. In understanding our various approaches, I find particularly helpful William Hasker's distinction between general-policy theodicies and specific-benefit theodicies. I take it that Hasker and Thomas Oord's approaches are general-policy theodicies, whereas those of Phillip Cary, Stephen Wykstra, and myself are specific-benefit theodicies or, at least, defenses. That is to say, we three believe that God has specific reasons for allowing this or that evil to occur, even if those reasons remain unknown to us. As Hasker points out, there is no inconsistency between these two approaches; indeed, I see a Molinist perspective as filling out a general-policy approach. I was pleasantly surprised to discover that nothing in Hasker or Oord's general-policy theodicies entails that God lacks middle knowledge, so that those theodicies could be extended to include specific benefits as well. It would be wonderful and welcome if a general-policy theodicy can alone and without extension succeed in turning back the force of probabilistic internal and external statements of the problem of evil, and I wish my colleagues well.

I see a Molinist perspective as being a classic view, as described by Cary. "The basic answer to the problem of evil given by the classic view is that no evil takes place unless God permits it, and that God has a good reason for permitting each evil." A Molinist version of the classic view enjoys the advantage that it provides an account of the second part of Cary's greater-good principle, according to which God "freely chooses to permit evils he could have prevented, because in his wisdom he knows how to bring a greater good out of precisely these evils." He knows this by means of his middle knowledge.

I also agree with Cary's claims about the ontological status of evil as a privation and, therefore, not something created by God, and about the origination of moral evil in the creaturely will's turning away from God, the supreme Good, to lesser goods. One need not break one's head about how the creaturely will can first become thus disordered if one believes in libertarian freedom, for if the will is free there can be no efficient cause of one's freely choosing. So Augustine's admonition, "Let no one therefore seek the efficient cause of an evil will," quoted by Cary, is wholly justified.

Less helpful is Cary's claim that the answer to the question why God makes creatures that are corruptible "is that if there is to be creation at all, there is no alternative to corruptible things, because all creatures are by nature corruptible." For this sits uneasily with his later claim that in the eschaton "we will be as unable to sin as our bodies will be unable to get sick or die." Even if one tries to explain the seeming inconsistency by appealing to the contrast between nature and grace, still it turns out that there is an alternative to corruptible things after all. The answer to the question why God made corruptible things cannot be that it belongs essentially to creatures to be corruptible, unless one gives up the view that in the new creation we will be unable to sin and to get sick or die.

The classic (Molinist) view is also a version of what Wykstra calls "sensibly humble theism." Molinism makes such a circumspect theism eminently plausible by means of its doctrine of middle knowledge, which makes it perspicuous why we should not expect to discern God's reasons for allowing various evils in the world. I found especially insightful Wykstra's distinction between "It does not appear that p" and "It appears that not-p." As he illustrates, what one takes to lie within the scope of the negation can make an enormous difference. As a result of reading his essay, I realized that I had myself fallen into the trap of which he warned. For in dealing with the external problem of evil, I wrote, "The theist will readily admit that much of the evil we observe in the world appears to be pointless and unnecessary and, hence, gratuitous. But he might challenge the objector's inference from the appearance of gratuitous evil to the reality of gratuitous evil." I conceded too much, admitting, in effect, that "it appears that much of the evil in the world has no point," when I should have at most agreed that "it does not appear that much of the evil in the world has a point." Given God's middle knowledge, it most definitely does not appear that that much of the evil in the world is pointless, for as Wykstra emphasizes, we're in no position at all to make such a judgment.

I obviously resonate with Wykstra's treating mere theism as the hard core of a worldview research program, for my adding to mere theism various auxiliary hypotheses drawn from a Christian worldview in order to increase the probability of evil on theism is an instance of such a richer perspective. My approach, though a sensibly humble theism, should not be called skeptical theism, because I think that we have good reasons to believe that Christian theism is true.

That brings us to Oord's approach. Oord would solve the problem of evil by maintaining (1) that it is impossible for God to withdraw, override, or fail to provide the freedom, agency, or basic existence of others; and (2) that it is impossible for God to interrupt or interfere with the law-like regularities of existence. The fundamental problem with this theodicy is that it is useless to the Christian because the view it entails is not Christianity. We should call it for what it is: deism. Indeed, it is deism of a very radical sort. The typical deist will affirm the existence of such a noninterventionist deity, one who first brought the world into being and now conserves it from moment to moment, but I know of no classical deist who would affirm with Oord that God is essentially incapable of intervening in the world.

Such a view is manifestly unbiblical. To give just one small example of God's apparently nonmiraculous intervention, consider how God prevented Jesus' falling victim to King Herod's murderous intentions following the departure of the magi: "Behold, an angel of the Lord appeared to Joseph in a dream and said, 'Rise, take the child and his mother, and flee to Egypt, and remain there till I tell you; for Herod is about to search for the child, to destroy him'" (Mt 2:13 RSV). This was not a miraculous angelic appearance, interrupting or interfering with the law-like regularities of existence; Joseph merely had a dream. So does this count as God's *overriding* Joseph's free will? If we take such involvement in human affairs to constitute an infringement of human freedom, then Oord's view is plainly unbiblical, as God is frequently described in Scripture as interacting with human agents to direct the course of events. If it is not an infringement of human freedom, then Oord's view does nothing to explain why God did not similarly warn the other parents in Bethlehem, whose children perished by Herod's sword, or act to prevent innumerable other evils.

As for God's miraculous interaction with human people, consider the following scene from Jesus' arrest in the garden: "When those who were about him saw what would follow, they said, 'Lord, shall we strike with the sword?' And one of them struck the slave of the high priest and cut off his right ear. But Jesus said, 'No more of this!' And he touched his ear and healed him" (Lk 22:49-51 RSV). Here Jesus interferes with a law-like regularity to undo an evil freely perpetrated by one of his disciples. It would be easy to multiply such biblical examples of God's miraculous activity, with or without human intermediaries. A general-policy theodicist like Hasker will emphasize that such interventions on God's part cannot be frequent or expected, lest the general policy be undone by such interventions; but the idea that God is essentially incapable of interfering with secondary causes in the world is wholly at odds with biblical theism. Indeed, such a view rules out the incarnation and resurrection of Jesus, and much else besides.

Moreover, Oord's view is philosophically and theologically untenable. Theologically, the view entails a woefully inadequate doctrine of divine providence. Indeed, the view amounts to a denial of divine providence altogether, since absent middle knowledge there is no way a God who is essentially incapable of interfering with free agents or law-like regularities of nature can guide the world. So far as providence is concerned, Oord's deism does not differ from naturalism. Oord's uninvolved deity makes Hasker's God look like a busy beaver, for at least he is actively engaged in the struggle against evil!

Philosophically, it is dubious that Oord's theodicy is successful even as a defense of deism. Indeed, does not the problem of evil itself pose an insuperable objection to Oord's deism? God, on Oord's view, refuses to get involved in human affairs so as to warn people of impending dangers or to move someone to prevent or rescue another person from suffering. He stands idly by, doing nothing to help, with no good reason for his noninterference.

Even if God is incapable of interfering with nature's law-like regularities, presumably he at least freely chose in the first place the laws of nature that are in force. But then Oord's deity must bear the responsibility for choosing laws that would issue in creatures so vulnerable to natural evil, rather than choosing other laws or refraining altogether from creation.

On Oord's view God does not lack the raw power to interfere in the course of human affairs or in the course of nature so as to prevent or remedy evils. Any being capable of creating and sustaining the universe in existence must have the power so to act. Rather, God's essential inability to interfere with law-like regularities stems from his moral nature. He loves and respects the created order so much that he cannot intervene. But any deity that is essentially such that it values the regularity of the laws of nature above the well-being of human people cannot in any recognizable sense be called good. Oord's God does not love Amy Monroe enough to interfere with the regularities of nature as she is raped and strangled. In the US criminal justice system Oord's deity, due to his "depraved indifference" and "reckless endangerment," would be guilty of crimes such as manslaughter and even murder. Does Oord seriously think that making such properties essential to God does anything to solve the problem? Oord's deity is essentially reckless and depraved, which is to say that he is not good. The very fact that Oord's deity values the laws of nature above the interests of people is proof positive that such a being is not, despite Oord's asseverations, really loving, for he values things above people, which is perverse.

So what will we say? If we are to preserve God's goodness, then we cannot say that he is essentially such that he values the regularity of nature over the well-being of people. The general-policy strategist must rather revert to Hasker's view that God voluntarily prescinds from frequently intervening in the world to prevent evil. But then Oord's objections to such a voluntary self-limitation on God's part do press hard on Hasker. With respect to natural evil, I think Hasker needs to say more in response to the question "Is a world that has unfolded in this way *better* than if, as our fathers believed until very recently, the major features of the universe, and each separate kind of living creature, had been handcrafted, as it were, by the Creator?"

The awe and wonder at biological evolution that is expressed by the authors Hasker cites masks the tremendous cost at which it seems to be bought. Suffering is not just an accompaniment of biological evolution; it is essential to it and drives it forward. Philip Kitcher makes the point in florid language:

> Many people have been troubled by human suffering, and that of other sentient creatures, and have wondered how those pains are compatible with the designs of an all-powerful and loving God. Darwin's account of the history of life greatly enlarges the scale on which suffering takes place. Through millions of years, billions of animals experience vast amounts of pain, supposedly so that, after an enormous number of extinctions of entire species, on the tip of one twig of the evolutionary tree, there may emerge a species with the special properties that make us able to worship the Creator. Even though there may be some qualitative difference between human pain and the pain of other animals, deriving perhaps from our ability to understand what is happening to us and to represent the terrible consequences, it is plain to anyone who has ever seen an animal ensnared or a fish writhe on a hook, that we are not the only organisms who suffer. Moreover, animal suffering isn't incidental to the unfolding of life, but integral to it. Natural selection is founded on strenuous competition, and although the race isn't always to the ruthless, there are plenty of occasions on which it does produce "nature red in tooth and claw" (in Tennyson's pre-Darwinian phrase). Our conception of a providential Creator must suppose that He has constructed a shaggy-dog story, a history of life that consists of a three-billion-year curtain-raiser to the main event, in which millions of sentient beings suffer, often acutely, and that the suffering is not a by-product but constitutive of the script the Creator has chosen to write.[1]

Why think that a world that unfolds like this is better than the world of the young earth creationist?

With regard to Hasker's ad hominem consideration, I doubt that "nontheists are likely to find it awkward to insist that it would be much better for the world to have been created by a complex series of specific divine actions, rather than allowed to evolve naturally." I do not see that it is awkward for a nontheist to think that if God existed, he should or would probably create the biological realm de novo rather than through so painful

---

[1]Philip Kitcher, *Living with Darwin: Evolution, Design, and the Future of Faith* (Oxford: Oxford University Press, 2007), 123-24.

a process. Yes, biological evolution offers "some help with the problem, by showing a beneficial result from the pain and suffering that exist in the natural world." But that does not answer the original question Hasker posed.

There can be good reasons, I think, for God's using a long evolutionary process to create human beings. For example, the fossil fuels that make civilization possible are the residue of vast primeval forests that flourished for eons in the past. A viable ecosystem would include animals that were part of that system. All things being equal, a world with a genuine past seems preferable to a magically produced world with the appearance of age. Still, something more needs to be said in order to justify Hasker's assertion that "the natural order theodicy contends that the price was worth paying."

I think that Michael Murray's work on the problem of animal pain can be of help to the general-policy theodicist by reducing the cost at which an evolutionary past is purchased. While Kitcher makes passing reference to the "qualitative difference between human pain and the pain of other animals," he does not really take it seriously. In his book *Nature Red in Tooth and Claw: Theism and the Problem of Animal Suffering*, Murray distinguishes three ascending levels in a pain hierarchy:

Level 3: a second-order awareness that one is oneself experiencing

Level 2: a first-order, subjective experience of pain

Level 1: information-bearing neural states produced by noxious stimuli, resulting in aversive behavior

Spiders and insects experience level (1). But there is no reason to attribute level (2) to such creatures. It is plausible that they are not sentient beings at all, having a subjective, interior life of some sort. Sentient experience plausibly does not arise until one gets to the level of vertebrates in the animal kingdom. But even though animals such as dogs, cats, and horses experience pain, nevertheless the evidence is that they do not experience level (3), the awareness that they are themselves in pain. For the awareness that one is oneself in pain requires self-awareness, which is missing in all animals except perhaps for the humanoid primates. Thus, remarkably, even though animals might experience pain, they are not aware of being themselves in pain.

Murray finds an analogy to animals' experience of pain in the remarkable phenomenon of blind sight. Blind-sighted persons have no awareness of being able to see; they are for all practical purposes blind. And yet they actually can see! They will catch a ball thrown to them or avoid a chair if asked to come across the room. They can see, but they are not aware that they can see. Similarly animals, though in pain, are not aware that they are themselves in pain.

God in his mercy has apparently spared animals the awareness of being themselves in pain. Thus their suffering is of a wholly different character than ours. Murray points out that we humans have an inveterate tendency toward anthropopathism, that is, projecting human states of mind onto animals (like William Rowe's fawn) and even inanimate objects. This makes the problem of animal suffering indistinguishable from that of human suffering, when in fact they are importantly different. Such an understanding of animal pain can help to justify Hasker's claim that the evolutionary process was worth the price.

As I say, I want a general-policy theodicy to work, even though I think that there are specific benefits to justify God's allowing suffering and evil. Remember, we are not doing systematic theology here but apologetics, trying to defeat an objection to theistic belief. A general-policy theodicy will not provide an adequate doctrine of divine providence, but it will be consistent with such a doctrine, unless, as in the case of Oord's theodicy, it precludes a God who is directly involved in his creation.

8

The Open Theist Response

WILLIAM HASKER

I want to begin by thanking my fellow contributors for their thoughtful, deeply considered reflections on an extremely difficult problem in philosophy and theology. Each of the contributions reveals concentrated thought on the issue, and each contains valuable insights and ideas. Furthermore, each of the perspectives has proved its usefulness by bringing a degree of comfort and resolution to some people wrestling with the problem of reconciling the evils of this world with the existence of a good and loving God. Nevertheless, as the saying goes, "the truth is out there," and it is now my task to explain why, in my estimation, open theism offers the best solution to the problem of those on offer here.

I want first to say something about the opening section of Stephen Wykstra's essay, in which he confronts us with his own loss of his father and with Nicholas Wolterstorff's grief over the death of his son Eric. Wykstra performs a good service here, by reminding us of the human and existential context of our concerns over evil. Lacking this engagement, our philosophical ruminations on the problem can easily become formal, abstract, and far removed from the struggles of human life. But, as several of us have observed, there is a distinction between the "pastoral" (or emotional, or existential) problem of people struggling to make sense of suffering and evil in their lives and the lives of others close to them, and the philosophical problem of showing the congruence (or at least compatibility) of the existence of evil with the existence, power, and goodness of God. These are not the same problem, and while the pastoral problem should not be absent from our thoughts, our main concern in these pages must be with the philosophical problem.

We begin with Phillip Cary's "classic" response to the problem. Cary performs a valuable service by reminding us of some themes that are important in the treatment of evil by classical theologians but are less prominent in recent writings on the topic. For example, it is important to realize, in the light of the doctrine of creation, that every being created by God is in itself good, that evil is not a thing in itself (as it was for Augustine's Manichaean opponents) but rather a defect or corruption in what is essentially good and valuable. To be sure, it is possible to make too much of this point. Evil is indeed *no thing*, but that does not mean that it is *nothing*, unreal and therefore negligible, something we need take no serious account of. HIV, as a virus, might be in itself a good thing, ontologically speaking, but it is capable of doing enormous damage to human bodies it infects.

The main problem I have with Cary's account is his pervasive lack of clarity about the nature of free will. The basic question here concerns the difference between *compatibilist* accounts of free will and *incompatibilist* or *libertarian* accounts. On a compatibilist account, a person's will is free just in case she is able, in a given situation, to do whatever it is she most wants to do. (There are complications and refinements here, but we will pass them over since they don't affect the basic point at issue.) It does not matter whether one's choice and one's action are determined by prior causes, so long as those causes do not prevent the agent from doing whatever it is she wants to do. A person who stays in a room because the door is locked from the outside (as in a prison) *lacks* free will in this sense; a person who remains in the room voluntarily *has* free will, even if it is entirely inevitable, in the light of her previous life and her character, that she will choose to remain. The important point here is that this sort of free will is entirely *compatible* with the existence of prior causes that *guarantee* that she will act in this way and in no other. Libertarian (or incompatibilist) free will, in contrast, means that it is *entirely possible*, in a given situation, for a person to do any of two or more different things, even taking into account everything about the person's character and prior experience, as well as all the circumstances that obtain. This sort of free will, then, is *incompatible* with the person's choice in that situation being determined by prior causes. In particular, it is incompatible with the existence of divine decrees that predetermine that a person will act in a certain way.

Now, Cary has quite a bit to say in his essay about the will, but so far as I can tell he says nothing that is decisive between these two very different views on the subject. At this point, then, I am forced to make an interpretive decision. In making this decision I take my cue in part from the fact that Cary's major patron in his exposition is Augustine, who in his mature works was unquestionably a compatibilist and a determinist, affirming that everything that takes place occurs because of God's eternal decision that it will be so. Cary never himself says this in so many words, but so far as I can tell what he does say is congruent with this Augustinian view, and there is nothing that affirms or clearly suggests a libertarian view of free will. So that is how I will interpret him, and I will refer sometimes to his "Augustinian view" on the problem of evil. (If I have misinterpreted Cary, I hope that at some point he will make his understanding of this topic plain.)

Readers of my essay in this volume will already know that I see no hope for a deterministic approach as a solution to the problem of evil. The God who determines everything that happens in our world by efficacious decrees is not and cannot be the loving and just God of the Bible and Christian faith. I say this while recognizing that some very great theologians have been committed to a deterministic view. They were, I believe, simply wrong about this—and note that Augustine's doctrine of predestination prompted resistance right from the time when it first appeared. One comparatively minor point concerns God's "permission" of evils. Cary's essay is full of this language, but I don't think he is entitled to it. Calvin is much more forthright (see the quotation in Oord's essay): with an all-determining God, it makes no sense to distinguish between what God "permits" and what he wills—or, as we should also say, what he intends. God, facing no constraints other than that of logical consistency, has *deliberately chosen that every instance of sin and evil should occur exactly as it does occur*, and has taken all the steps necessary to *guarantee* that this will happen. The persons who commit the sins are fully responsible and guilty for them (and some will suffer in hell eternally because of them), even though there was never any real possibility that they would do otherwise. And on the other hand God, who is the author of this drama, is entirely free of any guilt or responsibility for all the evil he has caused to occur. If you, my reader, find this to be compatible with what you believe about the loving and just nature of our God, I can only shake my head sadly and turn away. A further point here: On this supposition, we must assume that *God is entirely pleased and delighted with everything that occurs on earth*; otherwise there would be an inner inconsistency in God's mind that is simply unthinkable. The Bible, in contrast, makes it abundantly clear on many different occasions that God is *not at all* pleased with some of the things that happen; it's hard to think of anything in the Bible that is more clear than that!

Next we turn to William Craig's Molinist view. An obvious but nevertheless important point here is that this view can be correct only if Molinism—the theory of divine middle knowledge—is itself true. I mention this because a majority of philosophers, including Christian philosophers, who have considered this question think this theory is not true. In particular, they think there are no true "counterfactuals of creaturely freedom," the propositions that, according to the view, make up the core of God's middle knowledge. With regard to a possible free choice that is never actually made, there are truths about what the creature *might possibly do* in that situation, and perhaps truths about what she *would probably do*, but there is no truth stating what she *would definitely do*. This is not the place to pursue that argument, but I can't help but ask: In Craig's fascinating scenario of the "hand of cards" dealt to God, *who or what is it that deals the cards*? God can't deal the cards to himself, but there doesn't seem to be anybody else who would be up to the job. (Indeed, in the precreation situation, there is nobody else in existence at all.) Maybe the cards can be shuffled in such a way as to be "superrandomized," made so utterly random that even God can't predict the outcome. If that could be done, God could simply draw from the pack. But I must leave it to Bill Craig to fill out that story for us.

Molinism is far better placed than Augustinian determinism to deal with the problem of evil, because Molinists do affirm libertarian free will. Adam and Eve ate the forbidden fruit, not because God had efficaciously decreed that they should do so but because they freely chose this course of action, having been fully able to refuse the serpent's temptation. Nevertheless, God does retain a very high degree of control over everything that happens. God might have preferred a history in which, under exactly those same circumstances, they would have refused the fruit. That history, however, is not available to God, because the counterfactuals of freedom told him that if confronted with the situation they would succumb to temptation. But God nevertheless did place them in that situation, in the full knowledge that they would sin—and so also with each and every instance of sin and evil that has ever occurred. God deliberately chose this complete world-history (this "possible world," as philosophers say) in preference to every other possibility that was available to him, and took all the steps necessary to ensure its exact realization. God, we might say, could not get everything he might want, but he could be absolutely certain of getting exactly what he planned for.

One consequence of this is that, for Molinism as for Augustinianism, the language of "permission" is really out of place as applied to God; it is too weak to cover the situation. God *deliberately chose this particular world-history, with each and every instance of sin and evil it contains, and took the needed steps to ensure its exact realization.* To say that God "did not intend" the evil events included in this history is to strain language beyond the breaking point. God *did specifically intend* the Holocaust, Hurricane Katrina, and whatever other instances of egregious evil might come to your mind. To deny this is to trifle with words.

Another consequence of this is that the Molinist is virtually forced to affirm the "greater-good" principle, which states that each and every instance of evil is a means to a greater good (or to the prevention of an equal or greater evil) that *even God could not obtain* without there being that evil, or some other evil as bad or worse. Otherwise, why was that evil included in God's plan? And this is where the philosophical problem of evil really begins to bite. For certainly it seems to all of us that there are many, many instances of evil in which no such greater good is forthcoming. These, then, would seem to be instances of "genuine evil," as Oord terms it—evil such that, all things considered, it would have been better if these events had never happened at all. But the greater-good principle is thought to be a necessary consequence from God's essential goodness; if that principle is violated, God is not good after all—or, perhaps, there is no God.

In this context, it becomes virtually inevitable for the Molinist to insist that we are not in a good position to judge whether various evils will have a sufficiently good result to justify their existence. I don't know whether Craig applies the label "skeptical theist" to himself, but there is much in his essay that points strongly in the direction of the sort of skeptical theism elaborated by Stephen Wykstra.[1] And that will be our next topic.

In addressing Wykstra's essay, I will focus on the second part, where he presents the response of skeptical theism to evidential arguments from evil of the type presented by William Rowe.[2] The basic outlines of what is going on here are clear enough. Rowe has argued,

1. There exist instances of intense suffering that an omnipotent, omniscient being could have prevented without thereby losing some greater good or permitting some evil equally bad or worse.

2. An omniscient, wholly good being would prevent the occurrence of any intense suffering it could, unless it could not do so without thereby losing some greater good or permitting some evil equally bad or worse.

3. There does not exist an omnipotent, omniscient, wholly good being.[3]

Now, the skeptical theist typically accepts (2), so in order to avoid the atheistic conclusion (1) must be denied. But everyone will admit that there are cases in which it *seems to us* that (1) is true; it seems that there are genuine evils, often taking the form of intense suffering, that lead to no greater good.

---

[1]Limitations of space prevent me from saying very much about Craig's suggestion that God might have permitted a great deal of suffering in order to further the growth of Christianity. This of course would hardly be impressive to non-Christians, nor does Craig claim that it would be. But even for Christians, I suspect that this suggestion can do only a small part of the needed work. The connection between suffering and Christian faith might exist, but it does not seem to function very reliably. Much suffering has occurred in times and places where the Christian gospel was unknown; this suffering can't have led at all directly to the promotion of Christian faith. Craig speaks of the "indulgent West," where the growth rates for Christianity are flat—but many European countries suffered terribly during the Second World War (Russia especially so), and no great revival of faith has been evident in those countries. And on the other hand the United States, which did escape many of the disasters that occurred elsewhere, probably has more active Christians in proportion to its population than any of those European countries.

[2]I must admit to being considerably puzzled by the concluding part of Wykstra's piece. Apparently the "expansionist theism" he wants us to consider consists of theism augmented by Christian beliefs concerning Jesus Christ, salvation through him, and the like. It seems that the version of the problem of evil in view here is the probabilistic argument from evil developed by Paul Draper. But we are never told in any detail what Draper's argument is, much less how the skeptical theist should respond to it. Rather, we find a discussion, well and good in itself, of how believers should respond when they find themselves unable to answer objections to their faith. It almost seems that Wykstra is conceding (at least temporary) defeat in the case of Draper's argument; he then turns to providing counsel for how we should respond in the face of this situation. But I don't know whether what I've said here really captures Wykstra's intentions.

[3]William Rowe, "The Problem of Evil and Some Varieties of Atheism," in Daniel Howard-Snyder, ed., *The Evidential Argument from Evil* (Bloomington: Indiana University Press, 1996), 2.

So the skeptical theist needs to undermine the evidential force of this "seeming," so that it no longer constitutes a good reason to disbelieve in God. As a means for doing this, Wykstra proposes

> DISPRO: If such a being as God does exist, what our minds see and grasp and purpose in evaluating events in our universe will be *vastly less* than what this being's mind sees and grasps and purposes.

I believe we should agree with Wykstra that, in accepting DISPRO, we remain comfortably within the boundaries of common sense. Even atheists should acknowledge the reasonableness of this principle. The question is how this fact bears on the evidence we seem to have for the truth of (1). At this point, the difference between two distinct types of skeptical theism becomes important; the two types can be termed *maximalist* skeptical theism and *moderate* skeptical theism. The difference between them concerns the extent to which the versions attempt to discredit the evidential force of the experience that seems to support (1). For a maximalist this experience, properly considered, has no evidential force at all. For the moderate, on the other hand, the experience is conceded to have some limited force, but force that is lessened sufficiently that it can reasonably be resisted, especially if one has already a fairly robust faith in God. In his earliest explorations of skeptical theism, Wykstra was pretty clearly a maximalist.[4] Recently he might have become more moderate, but I am not sure about this. What I will argue here is that (1) if skeptical theism is to achieve its objective, only the maximalist version will suffice; and (2) the maximalist version really is a seriously skeptical hypothesis, in precisely the sense Wykstra objects to; it forces us to deny something that all of us normally assume quite comfortably that we know to be true.

The inadequacy of moderate skeptical theism is shown by two objections; the objections are mutually independent but reinforce each other. The first objection was originally noted by Richard Swinburne.[5] He points out that, while it is true that our perceptions of good and evil are limited

[4]See Steven J. Wykstra, "The Humean Obstacle to Evidential Arguments from Suffering: On Avoiding the Evils of 'Appearance,'" *International Journal for the Philosophy of Religion* 16 (1984): 73-93.

[5]Richard Swinburne, *Providence and the Problem of Evil* (Oxford: Oxford University Press, 1988), 27-28.

in the way shown by DISPRO, *this principle by itself says nothing about whether the world is better or worse than we ordinarily take it to be.* It might be that there are indeed justifying goods for many or all of the evils that seem to us unjustified, and if that is true (1) might not be true at all. But it could equally well be the case that many of the evils for which we thought we could see a justifying good really are unjustified: either the evil is worse than we thought, or it has other bad consequences that are unknown to us, or the supposed justifying goods are less valuable than we had imagined. (Arguably some existing theodicies are guilty of precisely these mistakes.) In this case, there might be more unjustified evil than we suppose even in our darkest moments. Since DISPRO tells us nothing as to which of these options is correct, it does not significantly lessen the force of our evidence for (1).

But suppose we ignore these considerations and assume that the limitations noted by DISPRO really do cut in one direction only. Let's suppose, then, that with regard to any particular instance in which an evil seems to us to be unjustified, the reasonable supposition is that it is 90 percent probable that there really is a justifying good, only one that is unknown to us. Now at last it seems that the skeptical theist is in a good position. In an argument based on probabilities, where absolute certainty is unattainable, to have the chances of being right come out nine-to-one in your favor leaves you in pretty good shape. Unfortunately, this reasoning overlooks an important feature of the situation, namely, the *very large number* of apparently unjustified evils that exist in our world. If it were not for the desire to avoid Rowe-type arguments from evil, I believe almost any of us would naturally tend to agree with Oord that there are many, many instances of genuine evil in our world. And this changes the picture radically. If we assume that, for each such instance, the probability that the evil in question is justified is 90 percent, then for twenty-five such evils the probability that each and every one of them is justified shrinks to just 7 percent! And if God is to exist, given (2), *there cannot be even a single instance of genuinely unjustified evil.* Even if we (implausibly) set the probability that an individual evil is justified even higher, this higher figure will still be swamped by the accumulation of instances. And we are unlikely to run out of instances! The moderate version of skeptical theism just can't do the job.

In order to accomplish the objective, then, skeptical theism must be maximalist; it must insist that the experience which apparently supports (1) has no evidential force at all. But how can that claim be supported? The answer is simple but drastic: *We must assume that, in the light of the limitations indicated by DISPRO, we have no ability whatsoever to discern whether any particular event will have good or bad consequences overall.* We simply can't tell this; only an unjustified faith in our own competence blinds us to this fact. And if this is true, our impression that our experience supports (1) is an illusion. It's not that experience tells us that (1) is false. Rather, it tells us nothing at all concerning the truth or falsity of (1). But if that is so, Rowe's argument, and all similar arguments, fail because we have no rational basis for affirming a key premise.

We need to be aware, however, that the proposed move is drastic indeed. Michael Bergmann, a well-known maximalist, has acknowledged in discussion that, on his view, we have *no idea whatever* whether, on balance, the life of Mother Teresa is better or worse, makes a greater or lesser contribution to the goodness of the world overall, than the life of Saddam Hussein.[6] To be sure, Teresa's life is *morally* superior to Saddam's; that is easy to see. But which life is better overall is something we have no clue about.

This, however, comes in conflict with our ordinary moral reasoning. In many situations, though not in all, what we judge is morally right to do is determined by which action would, so far as we can tell, have better results than any of its alternatives. In so judging we assume that, for the most part and on the whole, what we are able to tell about the good or bad consequences of an action is a fairly reliable indicator of the action's real consequences. Not an infallible indicator, to be sure; surprises are always possible. On the maximalist view, however, *there is no basis whatsoever for this assumption we constantly make in practice.* Maximalist skeptical theism really is a seriously skeptical hypothesis. It is also a very difficult hypothesis to believe, once we reflect on Teresa and Saddam and many similar comparisons.

If skeptical theism is rejected, how can we counter Rowe's argument? My answer is straightforward: Rowe's premise (2) should be rejected. It's true that (2) (and even stronger premises) have been accepted by some Christian

---

[6]I have heard him do so on two separate occasions.

thinkers, but rejecting it is not an especially radical move; this principle has been rejected by such distinguished philosophers as John Hick, Austin Farrer, Michael Peterson, Marilyn Adams, Jeffrey Jordan, and James Sterba. And there is good reason to reject it, quite apart from the need to meet Rowe-type arguments. If we really, seriously believed that God would prevent any evil that did not have a greater good as its result, this would significantly undermine our own motivation to prevent or mitigate such evils. If I prevent some serious evil from occurring, I will actually prevent the greater good that, absent my interference, God would have brought about as a result of the evil in question. If, on the contrary, the evil would have no such good result, then God will not permit it, regardless of what I do or don't do. The fail-safe option, then, is to do nothing. But this is radically contrary to God's intention for us, as revealed in Scripture (consider the good Samaritan), so God would not adopt a policy that would have such a result. The full articulation of this argument, however, must be found elsewhere.[7]

Thomas Oord's "essential kenosis" view stands in many respects at the opposite pole from views affirming "total control" on God's part, such as the classical Augustinian view, or "near-total control," such as the Molinist view. In contrast to these, the essential kenosis view affirms *very little* control on God's part over what happens in this world of ours. It is no accident, I think, that Oord chooses to dialogue with open theist John Polkinghorne. Polkinghorne, more than many other figures in the history of Christian theology and philosophy, is in sympathy with some elements of Oord's position, and in view of this he is a congenial conversation partner. But according to Oord, Polkinghorne just doesn't go far enough. That is what we need to explore.

I am largely in agreement with the first four dimensions of Oord's solution to the problem of evil. I agree that God does empathize with

---

[7]See William Hasker, "The Necessity of Gratuitous Evil," *Faith and Philosophy* 9, no. 1 (1992): 23-44; Hasker, "Can God Permit 'Just Enough' Evil?," in *Providence, Evil, and the Openness of God* (London: Routledge, 2004), 80-94; and Hasker, *The Triumph of God over Evil* (Downers Grove, IL: IVP Academic, 2008), 191-98. An atheistic twist has been given to this argument by Stephen Maitzen in "Ordinary Morality Implies Atheism," *European Journal for Philosophy of Religion* 12 (2009): 17-26. Maitzen takes a principle similar to (2), which he claims is an entailment of theism, points out the conflict between this principle (assuming God exists) and ordinary morality, and draws the conclusion stated in his title. Theists, I assume, will find relinquishing (2) to be a more plausible way of resolving the conflict. For more on skeptical theism, see my "The Skeptical Solution to the Problem of Evil," in *Providence, Evil, and the Openness of God*, 43-57; and Hasker, "All Too Skeptical Theism," *International Journal for Philosophy of Religion* 68 (2010): 15-29.

sufferers—though perhaps not equally with all sufferers, such as those who suffer as a result of their own evil actions. Yes, God uses evil and suffering to teach us many things. And yes, God heals those who suffer, to the extent this is possible. And God does call us to be colaborers in overcoming evil. The difficulties mainly arise, as Oord anticipates, with regard to the "sovereignty" dimension of his solution. Oord's solution amounts in effect to saying that there is no instance in which God could prevent a genuine evil but refrains from doing so. If this is so, then there remains no problem of evil as Oord defines it—the problem of why God doesn't prevent genuine evil. The answer is, quite simply, "God can't." In order to give this answer, however, Oord has to very considerably restrict the power he attributes to God, in contrast with what is said in all versions (Calvinist, Arminian, Thomist, Eastern Orthodox, and so on) of traditional Christian theology. In response, I raise two questions. First, what is the rationale for this revision of the notion of divine power? Second, what in fact is God able to do in the world, given the restrictions as set forth by Oord?

Oord's answer to the first question is contained in the following words:

> God's nature of love makes it impossible for God to withdraw, override, or fail to provide the freedom, agency, or basic existence of others. God's giving of existence to others in love also means God cannot usurp the law-like regularities—what many call "the laws of nature"—we see at work in the world. Self-giving love is an aspect of God's eternal nature, and God cannot deny this nature.

This is *essential* kenosis." Oord rejects talk of God's "self-limitation," because this implies that God might have chosen *not* to be limited, and thus God would after all have been able to prevent genuine evils. But, we might ask, *why* should "self-giving love" prevent God from ever overriding the laws of nature? Oord quotes Wesley to the effect that God cannot take away human free will. But shouldn't love have a sense of proportion here? If God's "love" means that he values the existence of a virus—something that is not, by all accounts, alive at all—equally with the life of a human being, we certainly are going to wonder about the indiscriminate nature of such love! (We would have no patience for a parent who made a similar choice.) Love, we want to say, should be a rational choice, not just a blind determination to go on doing what one was doing, no matter what. That "God loves *all* creation" need not mean—and, I submit, should not mean—that God is unable to make discriminations of value between the parts of that creation.

But given the limitations imposed by essential kenosis, what *can* God do about what goes on in the world? This seem to me to be an important question, but it is one to which Oord fails to give us a clear answer. He tells us God can work miracles but fails to explain in his essay what he takes a miracle to be or how this relates to the inviolability of natural law. A particular concern is the nature of God's "call," or God's "leading," to which Oord refers. Is this call simply the "voice of conscience," which is (we think) part of the natural endowment of a human being? Or is God able to bring it about, without overriding anyone's free will, that people have particular thoughts and feelings that they would not have had if God were not specifically communicating with them? If he cannot do this, it is hard to see how we can attach any serious meaning to the notion of the inspiration of the Bible. If he can, could he not have "inspired" the passerby when Amy was being murdered to take her cry for help more seriously? But then, this might have involved a "usurpation" of the laws of nature that govern the thoughts that occur to us—supposing that there are such laws. Oord, however, sheds little light on any of this. I believe, in any case, that he is going to have a *very* long, steep, uphill climb in order to give any plausible interpretation of Scripture that accords with what he has said about God's power. But we can't pursue that issue in detail here.

In this response I have considered a range of options, all the way from a maximal version of God's control to a minimal version. It's my contention that open theism is sitting in the "Goldilocks chair," nicely balanced between the extremes. But that is a claim it seems unlikely we will reach consensus about.

9

The Essential Kenosis Response

THOMAS JAY OORD

I enjoyed reading the responses my conversation partners gave to the problem of evil. In what follows, I give brief musings on each response. But I begin with reflection on their responses as a whole.

I was struck by the appeal to mystery I found in these essays. I did not appeal to mystery in my essay, but I did admit to being unable to know all truth. I'm sure my fellow essayists would also claim to have limited understanding about truth. None of us have figured out God or reality completely!

To admit to not knowing all truth, however, differs from the appeals to mystery I find in the other essays. As I read them, the other essayists provide partial solutions and appeal to mystery on the crucial issue of God preventing evil. By contrast, I offered a full-orbed solution to the problem of evil, focusing especially on the issue of God's power.

Stephen Wykstra is the most obvious example of one who appeals to mystery. He admits that horrific suffering occurs, and we "see no good that makes it needed for the theistic God to allow." But "humans should not expect to see or grasp very much of God's purposes," he argues. The problem of evil is "beyond answers," which is Wykstra's obvious appeal to mystery.

The classic view, according to Phillip Cary, says that "every particular evil is one God could have prevented but freely chose to permit." The classic view asks us to assume that evil somehow and in some inscrutable way promotes greater good. How evil promotes the greater good is hidden to us; it is mystery. Consequently, says Cary, "hiddenness is essential to the meaning of our suffering."

William Lane Craig also admits that God permits evil that God could have prevented. "Everything that happens . . . occurs by God's will or permission and thus falls under his providence," says Craig. The reasons God permits evil "far transcend the foresight of any temporally bound person," he argues. "Many evils seem pointless and unnecessary to us," says Craig, "but we are simply not in a position to judge." Although Craig claims he is not appealing to mystery, I cannot interpret these words and many others in his essay as meaning otherwise.

William Hasker comes closest to offering a mystery-free solution to the problem of evil. But Hasker believes God *could* prevent evil and perhaps on rare occasions intervenes to do so. He thinks that God allows natural evils and allows some creatures the freedom to operate without direct control. "Frequent and routine intervention by God to prevent the misuse of freedom by creatures," Hasker argues, "would undermine the structure of human life and community intended in the plan of creation." All of this means that Hasker eventually appeals to mystery: "we *just do not know* why certain sorts of evils are permitted by God."

Careful readers will find that I do not appeal to mystery on this crucial issue of God preventing evil. I do not say God permits or allows evil that God could have stopped. I do not appeal to divine hiddenness or inscrutability. This makes my essay fundamentally different from the others.

Let me illustrate this fundamental difference and its implications:

Suppose while hiking the wilderness of Idaho I found a soda bottle with a message inside. Suppose someone from Nairobi, Kenya, wrote the message. After reading it, I might wonder how the bottle traveled such a great distance—half the globe—to my remote North American location.

Suppose we asked five people unaware of the bottle's actual journey to speculate how it departed Nairobi and eventually arrived in Idaho. And suppose we also assemble a panel of judges to read the speculations of the five people and assess which explanation is most plausible.

Suppose the judges read the five explanations and found that each guess differed in detail. One person speculated that the bottle traveled north out of Africa through Israel and eventually to the shores of France. Another speculated that the bottle traversed north and then east through the Asian continent to China's eastern ocean shores. Others offered their own guesses on how the bottle left Nairobi and traveled to an ocean. In addition, each of the five people differed on how they guessed the bottle traveled to Idaho after it arrived in North America. In sum, the judges read clever speculations about the routes taken and those who carried the bottle with its message.

Let us also suppose, however, that our judges found something surprising: only one person offered a possible account of how the bottle traversed the oceans on its way to North America. Four explanations completely left out any account of how the bottle traveled this crucial leg—across the earth's large bodies of water—on its journey to Idaho. Not accounting for this crucial segment of the bottle's trip seriously undermines the overall plausibility of four of the five explanations!

Now let me apply my bottle illustration to the essays in this book. My fellow essayists claim God permits or allows evils. They think permitting evil is mysteriously consistent with God's perfect love. They argue in this way because they presuppose that God has the kind of power that makes it possible to prevent evils unilaterally. My fellow essayists all claim that at least in some circumstances, it is hidden from us why a perfectly loving God permits evil.

As I see it, failing to give a good answer to why a loving God doesn't prevent genuine evil is like explaining how a bottle traveled from Nairobi to Idaho without accounting for how the bottle crossed the oceans. Plausible explanation of the bottle's journey must account for crossing the world's large bodies of water. Likewise, plausible answers to the problem of evil must account for why a loving God does not prevent genuine evil. As I see it, my essay was the only one to account for this central issue.

For the remainder of the essay, I offer brief comments on the other four essays.

Phillip Cary had the unenviable responsibility of summarizing the various dimensions of what he calls the classic view of theodicy. I think his description is a faithful account of the many and diverse reasons Christians have given for why God doesn't prevent evil. Cary also offers a faithful account of reasons for even the possibility of evil. A book-length description would have been better, of course, but Cary did an admirable job given the essay length constraints.

Those who have read my essay will not be surprised that I find the classic view unsatisfying. In addition to appealing to mystery and to saying God allows evil that could have been prevented, the classic view is problematic in a way Cary's essay portrays well. The problem: the classic view offers a convoluted set of responses that neither individually nor together provide a satisfying solution to the problem of evil.

The convoluted nature of the classic view is illustrated well by Augustine's contributions to it. According to Augustine, evil is the corruption or privation of a good thing. Notice that this description of evil has a difficult time describing events such as rape, murder, or genocide. These evils are events, not things. One of the main reasons the classic view seems so confusing to contemporary people is that the metaphysics it presupposes fails to account well for life as we live and now understand it.

More importantly, as Cary rightly notes, the language of the classic view is bewildering. Those who endorse it use confusing phrases, such as those we find in Cary's essay. They talk about "bad good things" and "evil goods." We find the bewildering view that "all moral evil is a kind of love."[1] And so on. Given this, it is not surprising Cary admits often that confusion easily arises in the classic view. Puzzles abound!

There are several other dimensions of the classic view that I find unsatisfying. But I'll refrain from additional criticism here because some of those dimensions appear in my criticism of the other essays.

Other than the middle-knowledge factor central to Molinism, I did not find William Lane Craig's account significantly different from most aspects of the classic view. Craig helpfully identifies the intellectual, probabilistic, and emotional versions of the problem of evil. Addressing the problem of evil through these dimensions is typical among contemporary philosophers and a strength to Craig's essay. But Craig's fundamental response to the problem of evil is not much different from the classic position, including its claims to mystery. When it comes to why God allows instead of prevents evil, Craig has no good answer.

If I were convinced that the Molinist account of God's middle knowledge—relying as it does on the issue of God's knowing counterfactuals—were true, I might see a slight advantage to Craig's proposal. If middle knowledge were true, we would be able to account for creaturely freedom

---

[1] I offer a strong and fuller criticism of Augustine's language of love and the metaphysics underlying it in *The Nature of Love: A Theology* (St. Louis: Chalice, 2010), chap. 3.

and affirm exhaustive divine foreknowledge. But I am unconvinced by the Molinist account of divine foreknowledge. So I don't think Craig's response to the problem of evil adds much to what one finds in other versions of the classic view.

Two other points from Craig's essay seem especially worth noting: one helpful and the other not. In his criticism of William Hasker's open theist perspective, Craig says, "It doesn't take a genius to see that certain terrible moral or natural evils are about to happen, and a cognitively limited Superman would often seem blameworthy for not preventing or stopping them." Craig is criticizing the version of open theism that says God cannot know with certainty that particular evils will occur, but God does have the power to prevent them.

I agree with Craig on this criticism. The open view's denial of exhaustive foreknowledge has the advantage of God's not knowing from all eternity which particular evils will occur. But Hasker's version of open theism, with its view that God has the power to prevent evil unilaterally, is susceptible to Craig's criticism that God should anticipate and therefore prevent evils moments before they occur. This is one reason my own open and relational view denies both exhaustive foreknowledge *and* that God can prevent evil unilaterally.

The general point in Craig's essay I found particularly unhelpful was that God causes or allows evil to make us or the world better. According to Craig, "Natural and moral evils are part of the means God uses to draw people into his kingdom." And "evangelical Christianity is growing at its greatest rates" in "those countries that have endured severe hardship."

I agree that God can use suffering. But such use becomes problematic if, as Craig thinks, God causes or allows evil. If God has this kind of power, one should rightly wonder whether God cares enough about the kingdom and growth of Christianity. A God who cared more and had the power to cause or allow evil unilaterally should cause or allow *more* evil. If the end of salvation is justified by the means of evil, God should make the world a more evil place!

By contrast, the vision of God I propose says God *uses* evil that God didn't foreknow and couldn't prevent. My view better supports the claim that God always opposes evil, while affirming that God works to squeeze some good out of the genuine evil God didn't want in the first place.

Now to Stephen Wykstra's essay. Given that my essential kenosis solution to the problem of evil is perhaps the newest and least familiar proposal in this book, some readers might think the older, classic view Cary describes is least like mine. In terms of the substance of the two views, this might be correct. But the skeptical theism view Wykstra presents might actually be least like mine.

Skeptical theism essentially gives up on the project of offering a theodicy. While I propose a full-orbed solution to the problem of evil, Wykstra does not even attempt a partial one. Perhaps my attempting a full solution would strike him as hubristic, although I hope my claim that I do not know all things keeps him from labeling me "insanely" so. But as I see it, a solution to the problem of evil susceptible to the charge of hubris seems better than no proposed solution at all.

Wykstra begins his essay by addressing William Rowe's arguments and Nick Wolterstorff's story. As I first began reading his paper, I found myself hoping Wykstra would unequivocally affirm genuine evil. The other essayists in one way or another appeal to some greater-good or overall-plan argument, which essentially means that the pain and suffering we experience serve some greater good or less bad than would occur if God intervened to prevent them. At various points, Wykstra mentions pointless evils. And the evils he sometimes describes are horrific.

Before long, however, I found in my reading of Wykstra that the horrific evils he mentions are, in his view, only pointless from a human perspective. "We find many occurrences of horrific suffering for which we see no good that makes it needful for the theistic God to allow the event."

Notice the "we see" portion of this quote. According to Wykstra's view, no horrific suffering is genuinely evil, in the sense that it makes the world worse than it might have otherwise been. Horrific suffering is only pointless from our point of view, not from God's. These words sum up the argument: "humans should not expect to see or grasp very much of God's purposes."

A number of issues from Wykstra's essay arise as problematic. I will address four.

First, Wykstra is offering a defense, not a theodicy. His defense *begins* with belief in God. Assuming belief in God up front undermines the central question of whether the problem of evil should challenge belief in God's existence. Those with predetermined answers aren't likely to take the challenge seriously. It's really not a problem, at least in terms of deciding whether to affirm God's existence. When it comes to reasons why God might *not* exist, the skeptical theist affirms her predetermined answer and then appeals to mystery when that answer doesn't meet the challenges.

Second, Wykstra's predetermination of theism's truth does not account for the *varieties* of theism, even the varieties among Christians. Some versions of Christian theism are more plausible than others. As I see it, that's one of the main reasons for this book! The problem of evil can and should help us discern better versions of Christian theology from worse ones.

Third, although Jesus Christ doesn't offer a theoretical explanation for the problem of evil, most Christians believe the revelation of God in Jesus Christ helps us grasp God's purposes to some degree. Jesus offers a profound witness to the steadfast, all-embracing, and perfect love of God. The portrayal of power we see in Jesus tends strongly toward servanthood, suffering, cooperation, humility, self-giving, and empowering others. To use my language, Jesus' kenosis points to an uncontrolling God of love. Because I cannot imagine Jesus standing by and allowing genuine evils he could prevent, I cannot imagine God doing so. As I see it, a Christocentric view tells us enough about God for us to think that, if possible, God would prevent genuine evils.

Finally, Wykstra claims he has extremely limited knowledge of God's purposes. But he *does* have enough knowledge to affirm that God exists. I find this problematic. Let me explain by talking about God's love and power.

The problem of evil pertains to two divine attributes that, as I see it, cannot be isolated from the many reasons theists affirm God's existence. Those two are God's love and power. If, for instance, Wykstra believes divine revelation (found in the Bible or elsewhere) provides adequate reasons to affirm that God exists, it seems likely that such revelatory activity would be motivated by divine love and accomplished with some form of divine power. As far as I can tell, in fact, all the major reasons that Christians give for belief in God are reasons that directly or indirectly pertain to God's love and power. Consequently, I find no good rationale for being skeptical about the core issues of the problem-of-evil argument, which directly concern God's power and love, while affirming other arguments for God's existence that also concern God's love and power.

I conclude this essay response with comments on William Hasker's essay. I was not surprised to find Hasker's view the most congenial to my own. We both think the problem of evil can provide a strong reason for disbelief in God. Therefore we both take it seriously and search for a full-orbed theodicy. We both think the lack of incontrovertible proof of the best solution to the problem of evil should not deter the theist's work to pursue a solution. We both think the sciences need to be engaged when discussing providence in general and the problem of evil in particular. Hasker and I both affirm versions of open and relational theology, although he simply calls his view "open theism." I agree with nearly every italicized or bulleted point of Hasker's essay. Given my different view of divine power, however, I'd interpret some points differently from how Hasker might intend them to be interpreted.

The major difference between Hasker's theodicy and mine is our different views of divine power. Because he believes God essentially has the power to intervene and control creation, we find numerous references in Hasker's essay to God's "allowing" or "permitting" evil. God can also "rule over his creation" and "intervene," should God so decide. Of course, this language makes the problem of evil insuperable, which is why he eventually appeals to mystery.

Hasker affirms the possibility of what he calls "special action by the Creator." As he uses the phrase, special action can involve God's intervening to override the autonomy or freedom of creatures. But "frequent and routine intervention to prevent the misuse of freedom," says Hasker, "would undermine the structure of human life and community intended in the plan of creation." Therefore, says Hasker, "such intervention should not be expected to occur." He also talks about "more frequent divine intervention" to prevent evil. This suggests that Hasker thinks occasional divine intervention occurs, in the sense that God controls creatures or events so as to bring about a desired result. Perhaps the miracles he has in mind are events such as Jesus' resurrection.

Of course, affirming occasional interruptions raises serious problems in Hasker's proposal. In much of the essay, he argues that God chose to create a particular kind of world with particular features that make possible free will, indeterminacy, structure, creaturely responsibility, and more. But if

God occasionally interrupts to fix some issue, one wonders why God doesn't interrupt more to fix more issues. If God occasionally intervenes, we are forced to point to atrocious evils that God didn't prevent and say, "Apparently that horror was not genuinely evil, because it did not warrant God's intervention."

Hasker's "overall plan of creation" theodicy doesn't claim that every particular horror in the world is somehow necessary in God's meticulous control of creation. Hasker doesn't think God created a world that needs constant controlling. That's part of the beauty of most open and relational theologies. But according to Hasker's version of open theism, the horrors God permitted must not be *genuine* evils, in the sense of making the world, all things considered, worse than it might have been. Instead, God apparently allows some horrors because stopping them would, in some way, throw the world process out of kilter or undermine our trust in the structures of existence. God apparently allows some horrors, because preventing them would be worse overall.

I find Hasker's "overall plan of creation" theodicy very similar to the free process defense that John Polkinghorne and others advocate.[2] The usual version of the free process defense says God voluntarily created a dynamic universe with various processes, conditions, and structures. The universe God created included the possibility of creaturely freedom, indeterminacy, agency, and a measure of spontaneity. These processes, with both their novelty and regularities, allow for pleasure and pain, health and suffering, good and evil. Hasker would likely agree.

I affirm the free process view, but my version is different in important ways. Polkinghorne's version of the free process view begins with God's sovereign will. It says God voluntarily self-limits in relation to creation, voluntarily giving agency, free will, self-organization, and so on. The voluntary self-limitation theodicy cannot answer well why God doesn't occasionally become un-self-limited, in the name of love, to prevent genuine evil. Voluntarily self-limitation theodicies fail to solve the problem of evil.

---

[2]For a nice overview of the free process defense, see Garry DeWeese, "Natural Evil: A 'Free Process' Defense," in *God and Evil: The Case for God in a World Filled with Pain*, ed. Chad Meister and James K. Dew Jr. (Downers Grove, IL: IVP Academic, 2013), 53-64.

Hasker's statements about God's intervention and capacity to prevent evil assume that God sovereignly decided to create a world with creatures possessing relative autonomy. Hasker also seems to assume that God's will logically precedes God's nature, at least when creating the world and perhaps thereafter. In his view, God could withdraw, override, or fail to provide autonomy to creatures. God's limitations are voluntary rather than essential to God's nature. Consequently, his overall plan of creation theodicy fails to solve the problem of evil, because he cannot answer well why God permits evil.

The conclusion to Hasker's essay is the least satisfactory portion of his proposal. In it, Hasker appeals to mystery when it comes to why God doesn't do more to prevent particular instances of evil. "We have little insight into what frequent intervention might mean," he writes. And "very often we just do not know why certain sorts of evil are permitted by God." For an argument to be made that avoids the appeal to mystery, says Hasker, "we should need the requirement that each individual instance of evil should lead to a greater good or to the provision of an equal or greater evil." But Hasker cannot account for each instance of evil. He believes, therefore, that we should wish "that God would do more to alleviate the evils that most directly concern us."

The God of essential kenosis, by contrast, is not culpable for evil in general or any instance of evil in particular. Rather than permitting or allowing evil—an activity that all other book contributors think God does— the God of essential kenosis works to prevent *every* instance of evil. God cannot prevent evil unilaterally, however, because God's nature is self-giving, others-empowering love.

The contrast between Hasker's proposal and mine, therefore, is crucial on the point that makes my essay fundamentally different from the others as well. My conversation partners all presuppose that God has controlling power. By contrast, I think God's love is inherently uncontrolling. For this reason, I can offer a solution to the problem of evil that avoids appeals to mystery, while my conversation partners cannot.[3]

---

[3]For a fuller explanation of what the uncontrolling love of God entails for solving the problem of evil, see Thomas Jay Oord, *The Uncontrolling Love of God: An Open and Relational Account of Providence* (Downers Grove, IL: IVP Academic, 2015).

10

The Skeptical Theist Response

STEPHEN WYKSTRA

My fellow essayists offer four theodicies—four explanatory *models*, I'll call them—aiming constructively to help us see God's reasons for not preventing more of this world's evils. My own essay aims only to block some recent and trenchant atheistic arguments from analytic philosophers, and my defensive model mostly says that if God does exist, then we should not much *expect* to see, in any fullness or detail, his purposes for not preventing more of this world's evils. Clearly there's a tension here. But might, somehow, my model serve for defense, even as theirs serve their more ambitious aims?

This win-win will work only if their models give but *partial* explanations—leaving large gaps to be guarded by mine. My response here is thus a first effort at gap spotting, focusing especially on assumptions that shape the questions one sees as needing to be addressed by a theodical model. Gaps arise when a model, by its assumptions, erases certain questions—which also, of course, can make invisible its lack of answers to those questions.

ON CARY'S CLASSIC-THEISTIC MODEL

Phillip Cary's essay should convict us all of the need for frequent restudy of those early Christian thinkers whose ideas we so often reduce to cartoon caricatures. Nothing in analytic philosophy matches the analysis of the *nature* of evil given by his triple-A team of Augustine, Anselm, and Aquinas. I'm glad, too, to see his list of classic theists including John Calvin. Calvin and subsequent Reformed theology stressed the "meticulous providence" embraced by Cary's model, and that model, in the "Hidden Reasons" section, has clear affinities with skeptical theism. The affinities would be deeper— and that section longer—if we could resolve one small apparent difference.

The difference concerns the controversial greater-good principle that Cary and I both embrace. The principle, put roughly, says that whenever God permits a genuine evil, God does so for some ample "justifying reason" involving some greater or outweighing good.[1] We differ, however, on a detail of that principle.

Consider a case where some good person P (God, a good angel, a good mother), for the sake of some positive good G, acts so as to cause or permit some seriously "negative" event E to occur. What *necessary* conditions are satisfied when G gives, normatively speaking, ample *justifying* reason for P's action? On my own view, one is a No-Other-Way Condition:

> G is ample justifying reason for an action permitting E to occur *only if* P had *no other way* to fully secure or promote G than by the action of permitting E or something in a comparably negative ballpark.[2]

Something like this No-Other-Way Condition seems to me an essential part of a good's giving one ample justifying reason for permitting an evil. If a doctor achieved the greater good of saving your life by amputating your legs, but knew he could have equally well done this by giving you a simple antibiotic, you wouldn't say he had ample *justifying reason* for the double amputation. You'd instead want him arrested.

Cary's model, however, seems to imply that the No-Other-Way Condition is dispensable. That God will "bring some greater good out of the particular evils," he contends, does *not* mean "that he *must* permit these evils for the sake of these goods." Even giving us "free will," he argues, didn't require God to permit sin: God could have fully gotten this good by giving us from the get-go the "glorious perfect freedom" that God's redeemed will have in heaven.[3] Cary thus seems to reject the No-Other-Way Condition.[4]

---

[1] For simplicity I here let "greater goods" include "preventings of worse evils."

[2] Here the "ballpark" might have a foggy boundary: a fully adequate formulation of the No-Other-Way Condition will need to allow for any essentially vague boundaries. Here see Lecture 6 of Peter van Inwagen's *The Problem of Evil* (Oxford: Oxford University Press, 2006).

[3] Cary's argument fails if God's bringing Adam-like creatures to the desired "gloriously perfect freedom" requires—as seems to me not implausible—their firsthand experience of his mercy and grace.

[4] Late in his essay, Cary admits a small "no other way" aspect to "the more beautiful story" strand in

I say "seems" because this might be the unwitting result of a shift in focus. Citing Marilyn Adams's important book, Cary wants his model to highlight those long-range future goods that are compensatory and redemptive *to and for* the *victims* of unjust evil.[5] For such goods, the model invites roughly this picture: If God *hadn't* seen a way to bring greater goods for victims out of the evil they've suffered, God *wouldn't* have permitted that evil—but this doesn't mean God allowed the evils *for the sake of those goods* (as if he willed the evils *in order to* improve the victims). Now a little reflection shows that goods playing such compensating and redemptive goods need *not* satisfy a No-Other-Way Condition. Focusing just on them can thus cause this condition to slip from view.

Here an analogy might help. Imagine a little boy who realizes he's left his teddy bear "Winnie" at a highway rest stop, and a mother who, despite his heartbreaking pleas to turn back, drives steadily on. Two things, let's imagine, figure in her choice. First, she wants to arrive in time to prepare her aging father for a hospital appointment where he'll learn the results of a recent biopsy. Second, she plans to buy her son a "new Winnie" in the hospital gift shop—while also helping him learn that people matter more than things—which, however, he also needs to take better care of. The aims she has for her son play important restorative and redemptive roles, but if we focus just on them, we find nothing that *requires* her to drive steadily on. But it's the goods intended for her father that play the key roles in her *motivating rationale* for letting old Winnie perish, and reflection confirms that for these goods to play this role, there must be no other lower-cost way by which she can fully achieve them. So here I see Cary's model as needing to become—like my geezer eyeglasses—more bifocal.[6] A mono-focus on restorative goods, losing sight of the No-Other-Way Condition essential to motivating goods, will erase our hardest questions—"If God is all-powerful, couldn't he have done it some other lower-cost way?"—and thereby make invisible some wide gaps in the classic-theistic answers.

---

in his model. But he hedges it as a mere "conceptual truth" applying only to certain "general kinds" of evils, and so fails to grapple with its role as a necessary condition on goods within the motivating rationale for God's permission of particular horrendous evils.

[5]For a good encapsulation see Marilyn Adams, "Ignorance, Instrumentality, Compensation, and the Problem of Evil," *Sophia* 52, no. 1 (2013): 7-26.

[6]For more on keeping these distinct, see Alvin Plantinga's discussion of Adams in the final pages of his "Supralapsarianism, or 'O Felix Culpa,'" in *Christian Faith and the Problem of Evil*, ed. Peter van Inwagen (Grand Rapids: Eerdmans, 2004).

ON HASKER'S OPEN THEISTIC MODEL

Hasker's open theism gives all theists a valuable big picture of the diverse ways in which human suffering is connected to various great goods of God's universe—including developmental goods to which the evolutionary sciences now give us access. Those sciences also fit the open theistic stress on God's being *in time*: for God, as for us, the past alone is settled and done, whereas the future is a not-yet that is still unsettled. This is in part because it depends on our future free choices, which aren't "settled" until we actually make them. While the *destination* might be divinely assured, the exact *path* to it is not.

On Hasker's version of open theism, that path will be shaped by our ongoing free responses to God's initiatives, in which God is a risk-taking participant in our lives:

> When God decides to bring about a particular situation, one that involves creatures in making free choices, it is impossible even for God to know with certainty how those creatures will respond; there is a genuine possibility that they will not respond in the way he intended and desired them to do. (Of course there is much in the Bible that indicates that this not only could but also often does happen.)

In Hasker's first word here—"*When*"—I see a key question for open theists. For how often *does* God make such decisions? Only rarely, at key turning points of world history? Or frequently, in daily hidden ways for each of us? Or something in between?

I read Hasker's model as embracing the "daily" option. So read, his model underscores the biblical view of God as Immanuel, God with us. Or better, God *In-It-with-Us*—where the "it" includes both our exhilarating white-water days and those darker passages through proverbial thicker creeks up which, if God is not In-It-with-Us, we are indeed without a paddle. If this is part of Hasker's model, I nominate it as its most valuable part—its MVP.

But is this MVP compatible with Hasker's fascinating thesis that open theism has the distinctive merit of allowing—indeed, requiring—an *exclusively* "general policy" approach to theodicy? As I understand his terms, a general-policy account explains God's permitting of some class of evils in terms of God's following some "general policy" to secure or promote certain goods, whereas a "specific benefit" account explains God's permitting of some *particular* evil by appeal to some specific benefit thereby achieved. Hasker's thesis is that on open theism, and on it alone, "theodicy has *no need whatever* to appeal to beneficial consequences from God's permission of specific instances of evil. If the evil in question is the result of a general policy that is itself good and wise, that is a sufficient answer to the problem."

And open theism is uncongenial with specific-benefit theodicy, for "in a great many instances God cannot know, with certainty, what the consequences of a particular course of action will be, so it is out of the question to make the justification of God's permission of some evil dependent on something that logically cannot be known."

I see real promise in Hasker's insight that in accounting for a whole class of events, a general-policy explanation can in principle render superfluous or otiose any specific-benefit explanations of each event in that class. But in that insight, it seems to me, lurk important new questions for both the general/specific distinction and for open theism itself.

For open theism, the new (at least to me) question is whether God, lacking certain knowledge of my future choice in some envisioned situation, will still have some probabilistic single-case sense of the "objective chance" of my freely deciding to go in one direction (in, say, the direction he desires) rather than the opposite. On this, I think sensible open theists might want to work out a yes position, for free choices are nevertheless clearly *conditioned by* one's past habitual behavior, one's character, and one's movement in the direction of repentance and seeking God's help in change.

For the distinction itself, the new question is whether a specific-benefit rationale and explanation for some divine decision will then also need to be construed in some decision-theoretic sense. Suppose, for example, that God decides to bring about some crisis situation in your life, knowing that if you respond well, you will through teachable repentance avoid much harm to yourself and others. But suppose, to God's dismay, you instead choose to respond with pigheaded obstinacy, giving sin an increased hold, with highly injurious results. Would a detailed "theodical" account of *why* God brought about the crisis situation count as a specific-benefit account?

An open theist might answer no—since the hoped-for specific benefits did not in this case materialize. But for Hasker's model, I think, the right answer is yes. For if open theism is true, God's decisions will be either—in the parlance of decision theory—"decisions under uncertainty" or "decisions under risk," and these divine decisions will be motivated by specific benefits of an intrinsically chancy nature—benefits like bringing about this crisis situation that "*will give Wykstra the best chance of getting on the right track*." And if this is so, any God *In-It-with-Us* open theistic model will cry out for specific-benefit theodicies, for on such a model God's daily decisions and directives reflect his finely tuned *situational* sense of the objective chances of our responding well or poorly to situations he decides to bring about. A fully adequate theodicy of God's decisions would then need to give answers to specific-benefit questions about those *specific* situational parameters—those specific but objectively "chancy" benefits and perils—that grounded God's risky-but-not-reckless call.

Since we finite humans will often lack access to such specifics, I find Hasker's model an ally of skeptical theism. If Hasker decides to embrace an *exclusively* general-policy approach to theodicy, his model will become less friendly. But he will then also be giving up that Immanuel God In-It-with-Us that is, as I read him, the MVP of his current model.

ON CRAIG'S MOLINISTIC MODEL

Craig's Molinistic model, a version of classic theism, aligns well with skeptical theism. Like Hasker, Craig sees God as permitting much evil for the sake of having a universe that includes creatures—both human and angelic—gifted with deep moral freedom. Unlike Hasker, his model sees God as securing this freedom in a risk-free way, by attributing to God what I'll call *hyper*omniscience, by which God has eternal knowledge of "*counterfactual conditionals of creaturely freedom*."

To digest what these are, consider that free choice you made yesterday in Burger King at 12:14 p.m. when you found that stray twenty-dollar bill.

"But wait," you interrupt, "I wasn't in Burger King yesterday at all."

Exactly right! Since it didn't *in fact* occur, let's call it a counterfactual situation. Still, it *might* have occurred: after all, God *could* have brought it about, putting you in a situation of having to freely choose whether to furtively take the twenty rather than seek out its rightful owner. So here is the Molinist's first claim: God knows for sure what your free choice *would have* been, if that situation *were* to have occurred yesterday at 12:14 p.m.

But that's just a warmup. God, the Molinist says, *also* knows what your free choice would be if he were to bring about that situation—or more precisely, every possible variant of that situation—a year from now, or at any other future time. Moreover, God hyperknows the same things about Artsky W., my twin brother. Granted, Artsky doesn't in fact exist: my mom's ovum didn't split up that way. But it seems like he's a metaphysically *possible* person—it seems, that is, like God *could* have brought about that egg splitting. And if so, then Molinism says God has hyperknowledge about what Artsky freely chooses in every possible situation *he* could ever be in.

And based on his eternal hyperknowledge of things, says the model, God decided eternally—prior to the womb of time itself—to *not* make that situation in Burger King yesterday an actual one. And similarly, based on his hyperknowledge of Artsky's free choices, God decided not to let Artsky be born into our actual world.

I've here rehearsed my understanding of Molinism because it bears crucially on my one reservation about Craig's paper—his deployment of Molinism against *probabilistic* arguments from evil. Craig thinks Molinism helps by giving a set of doctrines "that would tend to raise the probability of inscrutable evil *given* God's existence." That is, it raises the probability of inscrutable evil *conditional* on theism. If Molinism does raise this conditional probability, I agree it will help—for it will help show that the theistic hypothesis itself "predicts" that many evils will serve no purpose we can see. But it will do this only if it's true *both* that inscrutable evil has a high probability conditional on Molinism, *and* that Molinism has a high probability conditional on theism. I grant the first but have problems with second. To be sure, I can "imagine" worlds where I have a twin brother Artsky W.; I can also imagine never-never land worlds where Peter Pan, Wendy, and Tinker Bell exist. But even if such worlds are "possible," I see no reason to think God has hyperknowledge of what counterfactual creatures "in" them freely choose to do, for such things are not real enough for there to be *truths* about them for God to have knowledge of. I thus don't think Molinism has a high probability on theism or Christian theism, and indeed think it likely is false. Still, I'm glad Craig sees Molinism as a friend of skeptical theism. It needs all the friends it can get.

ON OORD'S ESSENTIAL-KENOTIC MODEL

Thomas Oord's "complete solution" to the problem of evil opens by changing the question: "Why does God *permit* evil?" must, he says, change to "Why does God *not prevent* evil?" I get this. It's false to say Elvis Presley *permitted* Hitler's 1940 invasion of France—for Elvis, being then in kindergarten, had total *inability* to stop Hitler. Similarly, Oord wants to say, it's false to say that God *permits* the genuine evils of our world—for God, on his model, has total *inability* to prevent them.

On the model, this of course isn't because God is short on power or knowledge the way Elvis was. It's because God is "essentially kenotic"—as the essence of a triangle is to have three sides, the essential nature of God is to self-limit by *uncontrolling* love toward all created things. As a playful analogy we might consider how good parents "let go" of now-adult sons or daughters, giving them full space to be themselves and do their own thing. Parents find this hard, but for God it flows from his essential nature, loving in an uncontrolling way that gives created things, as it were, *ontological space to "do their thing,"* in accord with the nature and agency with which he has— according to their kind—gifted each of them.

To see more deeply into Oord's strategy, and raise some worries, let's connect it to Hasker's insights into general-policy theodicy. For what Oord's model does, at bottom, is explain evils by attributing to God a general policy of never unilaterally butting in. Moreover, what makes this a wise policy, on Oord's model, is that it serves a certain global good. To love something is, after all, to desire and pursue the best for that thing, and never butting in is, in Oord's words, part of God's holistic "quest to promote overall well-being" of all created things. Now Hasker, recall, urged that a general-policy account of a *class* of events can, in principle, make it senseless to seek specific-benefit accounts of particular events within that class. This helps us see a key feature of Oord's explanatory strategy. For, on his model, God's nonprevention of a human predator preying on a nine-year-old girl—Carrie, let's call her—has the same explanation as God's nonprevention of a hawk from preying on a rabbit: God by his essential nature cannot unilaterally butt in. For this reason, on Oord's model, it is senseless to ask, "Why did you not prevent this?" of tragedies like the death of nine-year-old Carrie. The model "answers" such questions by erasing them.

My worry is that the model erases too much too quickly. As I see it, Oord's core insight is that a God who lovingly creates a universe of good things like ours must essentially "self-limit" so as—in *some* way and to *some* degree—let those things do their thing. But the crucial question should here be how—and how much—God's essence constrains God to dial back. Oord's model proposes that God must dial back *completely*. Extremes have a certain attractive simplicity, but do we see anything in God's "essential nature" that dictates so unnuanced a divine policy?

A more nuanced policy would, I think, fit better with other things affirmed by Oord and by Scripture. Oord, like Cary and Hasker, sees in created things a scale of complexity and value. If God's policy is attuned to the value of things, might not God—due to his essential nature—*sometimes have to* butt in? Might God not *sometimes*, due to his valuing people more than protons, give a quantum-nudge to some father's synaptic connection, giving him an inexplicable urge to go pick his daughter up from school, instead of letting her walk home as usual? There is merit in supposing that God can't *always* stymie predators in this way, but does reason—or our own experience—tell us that God's essential nature dictates that he can *never* do it?

I don't think so: like Cary and Hasker, I see God as far more active in shaping events. To be sure, this means that I will—like Job—often protest that he isn't active enough, or when he should have been. But am I—who haven't had that much practice in running a universe that is both law-like and providential—really in an epistemic position to judge how much, or when, that is?[7]

CONTRA CRAIG: THE NEGLECTED REFORMED CONCURSUS MODEL

Craig's several deprecating asides on John Calvin and Reformed theology have helped me rediscover my own tradition. Unlike Molinists and open

---

[7]Of vital importance here are the modal-skeptical considerations advanced by Peter van Inwagen in the final sections of his "The Problem of Evil, the Problem of Air, and the Problem of Silence," reprinted in *The Evidential Argument from Evil*, ed. Daniel Howard-Snyder (Bloomington: Indiana University Press, 1996), 151-74. On the thorny issues about why God doesn't intervene when we (or Jesus) would intervene, see my "Beyond the Impasse: Contemporary Moral Theory and the Crisis of Skeptical Theism," in *Ethics and the Problem of Evil*, ed. James Sterba (Bloomington: Indiana University Press, forthcoming).

theists, who see God as "achieving his ultimate ends through creaturely free decisions," Craig jokes that Reformed theologians favor a God who foresees that "libertarian free creatures" wouldn't be worth the trouble and who instead decides "to actualize a world in which he himself determines everything that happens." As seen by Molinists and open theists, he adds, God is "engaged in the same struggle against sin and suffering that we are"—in sharp contrast with "the all-determining God of Reformed theology, with respect to whom it becomes meaningless to speak of a difference between his direct and permissive will."[8]

Calvin does indeed find in Scripture a God who is more active in shaping events than we easily imagine. In the biblical narrative of Joseph's brothers murderously throwing Joseph in a pit to die, Calvin finds a God who does not merely "permit" their evil actions but who actively, directly, and intentionally shapes these actions. "You meant evil against me," as Joseph much later told his brothers, "but God meant it for good" (Gen 50:20 NASB). While Calvin's polemics against the permissive/direct distinction can be off-putting, serious Calvin scholarship shows them to be directed at misuses of the distinction by Epicureans and libertines of his own time. When we look beneath the polemics, we find Calvin—with "much subtlety and intuitive sensitivity," as Neal Judisch puts it—forging a "Calvinian Thomism" that refurbishes the distinctive *concursus* metaphysics pioneered by Thomas Aquinas.[9]

Let's call this the Reformed Concurrentist model. On the model, I am excited to find, Calvin fully affirms the creature-causative powers of created things—including the power by which human beings, gifted with "will," make choices. What the model insists—its core insight—is that there is a unique metaphysical relation by which, in the bringing about of *every* natural event/action in our universe, the Creator-causative role of the Creator "*co*-operates" or acts in *concursus* with the powers with which the creatures are gifted. But on the model, their causal roles and motivations remain different from God's. God's Creator-causal role does

---

[8]In contrast to Craig, Oord says Calvin is right on this point—but he then derives from Calvin's point exactly the opposite conclusion as does Calvin!

[9]Neal Judisch, "Calvinian Thomism: Providence, Conservation and Concurrence in the Thought of John Calvin," *Called to Communion*, March 13, 2009, www.calledtocommunion.com/2009/03 /calvinian-thomism-providence-conservation-concurrence-in-the-thought-of-john-calvin/.

"bring it about" that (say) Joseph's brothers would first murderously decide to leave Joseph in a pit to die, and then relent ever so slightly. But God's causal role does not, on the model, make this any less than 100 percent *their* deed. Nor does it mean that God was anything less than appalled by their wrongdoing. The Reformed Concurrentist model, then, enables Reformed theology to see God as actively sovereign in all events and actions, while still giving "secondary causes"—including human will—their due. It also enables Calvinists—along with Molinists and open theists—to see God as fully engaged in the struggle against injustice, sin, and suffering.[10] I thus commend Reformed Concurrentism as a neglected constructive model worthy of further exploration.[11] While Craig might have meant his remarks to Calvin for evil, God meant them to Calvin—and me—for good.

SKEPTICAL THEISM RECONSIDERED

Skeptical theism, aiming to block difficult atheistic arguments, can easily neglect the need for big-picture answers. I honor my friends' models for addressing this need. But those difficult arguments can also help us see questions—and gaps—that big-picture models sometimes hide. And these questions and gaps arise in the life of faith itself. Returning to Wolterstorff's *Lament for a Son,* I find this passage:

> Faith endures; but my address to God is uncomfortably, perplexingly, altered. It's off-target, qualified. I want to ask for Eric back. But I can't. So I aim around the bulls-eye. I want to ask that God protect the members of my family. But I asked that for Eric.

Of course you must ask God to protect them, I want to say—it's in the prayer our Lord taught us: "Deliver us from evil." But if God actively *does* that, must he not have some *particular* reason when he seems *not* to do it? And so we cry out, "Why didn't you, God, on *this* occasion?"[12]

---

[10]Here see Nicholas Wolterstorff, "The Wounds of God: Calvin's Theology of Social Justice," *The Reformed Journal* 37, no. 6 (June 1987): 14-22.

[11]For a starting point richly connecting Reformed Concurrentism to both history and current analytic philosophy, see Luke Van Horn's "On Incorporating Middle Knowledge into Calvinism: A Theological/Metaphysical Muddle," *Journal of the Evangelical Theological Society* 55, no. 4 (2012): 807-27.

[12]Nicholas Wolterstorff, *Lament for a Son* (Grand Rapids: Eerdmans, 1987), 70.

But if faith allows this cry, it must spread out to all other particulars. Just so, Wolterstorff's lament spreads out:

> How is faith to endure, O God, when you allow all this scraping and tearing on us? You have allowed rivers of blood to flow, mountains of suffering to pile up, sobs to become humanity's song—all without lifting a finger that we could see. You have allowed bonds of love to be painfully snapped. If you have not abandoned us, explain yourself.[13]

To cling to Immanuel God In-It-with-Us then exacts this price: that when we sit on the mourners' bench, all these hardest particularist questions come swarming in. When God sits with us, we interrogate him—and in his silences new questions swarm in. When the models of my friends seem to leave no gaps, it might be because they quash so many real questions. And by this conversation over models we thus glimpse a spiritual role for skeptical theism: of helping us toward that stillness wherein we might sense a Presence beyond all models.[14]

---

[13]Ibid., 80.
[14]I thank Nick Wolterstorff and Kelly James Clark for their helpful fireside feedback on a much-extended version of this essay.

Name Index

Subject Index

Finding the Textbook You Need

The IVP Academic Textbook Selector
is an online tool for instantly finding the IVP books
suitable for over 250 courses across 24 disciplines.

---

ivpacademic.com

EVIL ABOUNDS. AND SO DO THE ATTEMPTS TO UNDERSTAND GOD IN THE FACE OF SUCH EVIL.

The problem of evil is a constant challenge to faith in God. How can we believe in a loving and powerful God given the existence of so much suffering in the world? Philosophers and theologians have addressed this problem countless times over the centuries. New explanations have been proposed in recent decades, drawing on resources in Scripture, theology, philosophy, and science.

VIEWS AND CONTRIBUTORS

CLASSIC VIEW
PHILLIP CARY

MOLINIST VIEW
WILLIAM LANE CRAIG

OPEN THEIST VIEW
WILLIAM HASKER

ESSENTIAL KENOSIS VIEW
THOMAS JAY OORD

SKEPTICAL THEIST VIEW
STEPHEN WYKSTRA

God and the Problem of Evil stages a dialogue between the five key positions in the current debate. According to the classic position, associated especially with the Augustinian tradition, God permits evil and suffering as part of the grand narrative of divine providence to bring about the redemption of creation. Molinism modifies the classic view by adding God's middle knowledge to the picture, in which God has knowledge of what creatures would do in all possible worlds. Open theism rejects the determinism of the classic view in favor of an account of God as a risk-taker who does not know for sure what the future holds. Essential kenosis goes further in providing a comprehensive theodicy by arguing that God cannot control creatures and thus cannot unilaterally prevent evil. Skeptical theism rejects the attempt to provide a theodicy and instead argues that, if God exists, we should not expect to understand God's purposes.

Edited, with an introduction, by Chad Meister and James K. Dew Jr., *God and the Problem of Evil* hosts a generous and informative conversation on one of the most pressing issues in the Christian life.

CHAD MEISTER (PhD, Marquette University) is professor of philosophy at Bethel College in Mishawaka, Indiana. He is the author of numerous articles and books, including *The Oxford Handbook of Religious Diversity*, *Introducing Philosophy of Religion*, *Reasons for Faith: Making a Case for the Christian Faith*, and *The Philosophy of Religion Reader*.

JAMES K. DEW JR. (PhD, Southeastern Baptist Theological Seminary) is associate professor of the history of ideas and philosophy and dean of the College at Southeastern Baptist Theological Seminary.

ISBN 978-0-8308-4024-3

Apologetics

IVP Academic
Evangelically Rooted. Critically Engaged.

www.ivpacademic.com